D0072718

ARE THERE ANY GOOD JOBS LEFT?

≫≪

Career Management in the Age of the Disposable Worker

R. William Holland

Westport, Connecticut
London

Library of Congress Cataloging-in-Publication Data

Holland, R. William.
   Are there any good jobs left? : career management in the
age of the disposable worker / R. William Holland.
     p. cm.
   Includes bibliographical references and index.
   ISBN 0-275-99044-3 (alk. paper)
   1. Career development—United States. 2. Career
changes—United States. I. Title.
HF5382.5.U5H636 2006
650.140973—dc22   2006015397

British Library Cataloguing in Publication Data is available.

Copyright © 2006 by R. William Holland

All rights reserved. No portion of this book may be
reproduced, by any process or technique, without the
express written consent of the publisher.

Library of Congress Catalog Card Number: 2006015397
ISBN: 0-275-99044-3

First published in 2006

Praeger Publishers, 88 Post Road West, Westport, CT 06881
An imprint of Greenwood Publishing Group, Inc.
www.praeger.com

Printed in the United States of America

The paper used in this book complies with the
Permanent Paper Standard issued by the National
Information Standards Organization (Z39.48-1984).

10 9 8 7 6 5 4 3 2 1

*To my loving wife, Claudia, who read every word and
offered countless candid suggestions.
But always with tenderness beneath her honesty*

CONTENTS

PREFACE

THE GULF BETWEEN an idea and a completed book is too wide to get over in a single leap. It takes connecting across shorter distances with support from others. That is how *Are There Any Good Jobs Left?* came to be.

The idea occurred to me several years ago as I observed increasing numbers of workers being displaced from their jobs. These displacements were different from those that took place during the Great Depression. There were no bread-lines to feed the hungry or any public works projects to absorb idle labor. In addition, many of the displaced were members of the recently emerging white-collar labor force. These were people with college educations, experiences, and career expectations unknown a generation before. As workers became increasingly anxious about job security, corporations became more at ease with restructuring their workforces and more willing to accept the consequences of laying people off.

Conversations with friends and colleagues confirmed my sense that fundamental shifts were taking place in the American labor force. Some time later, it became clear that similar changes were taking place in other industrialized countries. What was happening to workers in America was one component of an interrelated global landscape. By this time an entire body of literature about globalization and its effects had surfaced, along with a debate about the future of jobs everywhere.

In some respects, the debate clarified the possible impact globalization would have on individual classes of workers. It has not clarified what individuals should and can do about it. This book explores the most recent evolution of jobs and the attendant methodologies for finding them. It is divided into two parts, Context (chapters 1–5) and Practical Applications (6–9).

Chapter One, "Globalization and Our Individual Career Options," is a discussion about how globalization shapes the way in which companies behave in the global marketplace and impact the career opportunities for individuals. Chapter Two, "About You, Me, and Roy," is a personal account of how my family and friends experienced the transition to a global economy. Our experiences demonstrate how easily one can be misled when using old paradigms to understand new phenomena. Chapter Three ("How Did We Get Here from There?") is an overview of the changes in the post–World War II American economy and the rise of the outplacement industry. Here we begin to take a close-up look at an actual networking group and how individuals manage transitioning from one job to another. In Chapter Four ("Are There Any Good Jobs Left?") we focus more specifically on the changing landscape of jobs in America and the threat being posed to the American worker. Chapter Five, "Race and Gender in the Job Search Process," begs the question about the continuing relevance of race and gender in the job search arena. While both issues are likely to fade in importance, certain vestiges of each could remain and lead to a suboptimization of the nation's human resources.

Part II focuses on more practical applications. It begins to bridge the gap between the existence of global forces and the actions individuals can take to survive and prosper. Chapters Six, "Résumés," and Seven, "Networking, Interviewing, and Negotiating," focus on the inner workings of the career management process and how it needs to change in response to globalization. Chapter Eight, "The Entrepreneurial Spirit," is a study of the issues one encounters when becoming an entrepreneur.

The final chapter, "Suggestions for Survival and Prosperity," addresses options for survival in the new economy. Included are some straightforward suggestions about personal finances in the face of job insecurity and about personal brand management.

For those who want to learn more about the global economy, additional details about career planning, or other subjects covered here, a Resources section is provided for your assistance. Everyone should be able to use this work to gain a better understanding of the forces at play; how we got here, and the personal life strategies we can use to move forward. From time to time readers will be referred to my website, www.rwilliamhollandconsulting.com, where they will find additional resources, how to contact me, and information about my blog, *Are There Any Good Jobs Left?* A newsletter is in the planning stages that will focus on topics of interest to the active career manager and job seeker. A special set of help aids are also available for the college audience. The need to clarify how individuals might respond to the threats and opportunities posed by globalization was the final connection to make *Are There Any Good Jobs Left?* possible.

For helping me bridge this last gulf, I would like to thank Steve Shipley, Jane Goldfine, Don Kratz, Jan Kays, Debra Dewbray, Todd Holland, Jaime Holland, Chuck Hays, Carol Cepesdes, Jess Womack, Bob Holland, Ruth Scott, Kesha Reed-McLean, Robb Holland, Kristen Cox, Pat McGettrick, Marianne Blair, Amy Edwards, Bonnie Spark, Debra Jensen, June Stokes, and others too numerous to mention.

I would also like to thank Dan Gross, my invaluable research assistant for his dedication and insight. Special thanks to Nick Philipson and his staff at Praeger Publishers for their enthusiasm, belief in, and input on the project. Finally, thanks to my agent, Sorche Fairbank at Fairbank Literary, for providing careful guidance through territory unfamiliar to me.

PART I

Context

CHAPTER ONE

GLOBALIZATION AND OUR INDIVIDUAL CAREER OPTIONS

ACCORDING TO THE Bureau of Labor Statistics (BLS), 43 million Americans were laid off between 1979 and 1995. Between 2001 and 2003 another 5.3 million got pink slips. More than likely, the numbers would have been higher were companies not able to reduce their payrolls by offering incentives for early retirement. A few decades earlier, who would have thought it would be more profitable in the long term to give people incentives *not* to work? When did workers become so disposable? In retrospect, the popularity of early retirement incentives and massive layoffs should have been a warning that something was seriously out of kilter, and that major changes were just around the corner.

Increasingly, companies are advertising their jobs as "stints" rather than as long-term career opportunities. Pension programs are becoming little more than employee-funded retirement savings accounts portable from one company to the next. Under the protection of bankruptcy laws, an alarming number of companies are walking away from long-standing pension commitments. Smart companies are beginning to restructure their compensation programs and jobs so as to retain only selected employees for finite periods of time. Technology is making it possible to do the same work with fewer people. And the loss of jobs to technology is not confined to the United States. In fact, in 2004, China lost more manufacturing jobs to technology than any other country.[1] Much of the work being done by workers in industrialized countries can be done at less expense by other people anywhere in the world.

The largest employer in the United States is no longer General Motors. That distinction has gone to companies such as Wal-Mart and Manpower with employment rolls that have swollen to over 1.4 million and 600,000, respectively. That a retailer and a temporary employment agency are now among the largest employers is testimony to how much America has changed in the last few decades.

A WORLD OF UNCERTAINTY

As companies are rethinking how work gets done and as people continue to be downsized, outsourced, and let go, many are left wondering whether there are any good jobs left. The question has relevance for receptionists and CEOs; for college freshmen and graduating seniors; for those in midcareer and those about to retire; and certainly for those in transition. What we look for in jobs and careers and how we prepare ourselves to get them helps establish basic patterns in our lives, such as spending time and money to attend college, and providing our children with resources to do the same. We believe education is a ticket for admission to a good job—one with security of employment, health care benefits, career development, and a pension program for retirement. However, a review of the American landscape reveals that how we earn our living has changed. Furthermore, it has changed right before our eyes and seemingly in no more time than it has taken us to bat an eyelash. The magnitude of the changes and the speed at which they have come at us appear to have turned our world upside down. The price of the admission ticket to good jobs has steadily risen while what we are getting for a return is less certain than ever before. As Thomas Friedman put it in his book *The World Is Flat,* we are in the process of a great leveling of the global economic playing field.[2] How we prepare ourselves as a society and as individuals to deal with these changes will have a dramatic impact on the quality of our lives.

If individuals (and organizations) understand the context in which these changes are taking place, they will be better prepared to survive and prosper. But survival and prosperity in this new era require a significantly different approach and level of understanding than many of us currently use or possess. That requires us to understand the context out of which these changes have taken place.

My sense is that people, especially Americans, are confused and uncertain. Many are struggling more than ever to make sense out of everyday events in the greater workplace. College students are trying to make career choices about areas of study, hoping that jobs will be available in their fields well into the future. At one time it was possible to find employment with a company and have every expectation of spending the better part of one's working life with that organization. Now students at some of our most prestigious universities are being told to expect their first job out of college to last no more than four or five years.

People in transition are looking for jobs in companies that are here to stay. They want stability. They want to work for organizations that are not desperately trying to outsource most of what they do to others. They ask whether their next job is safe but find out, all too late, that the new companies they join lay people off as well.

There is confusion about technology and its effect on jobs, especially in manufacturing. We read every day that manufacturing jobs are on the move.

General Motors has announced it is establishing a manufacturing capability offshore and eliminating over 25,000 jobs at home. Where is home? Is it really okay for a Chinese company to buy Maytag or an American oil company? Is there not an oil shortage? Why would we let them buy our oil? Is it actually our oil they are buying?

There is also confusion about things Americans thought were sacrosanct. Most did not know that companies like United Airlines could walk away from their pension obligations, or that many private and public pension programs are seriously underfunded. Few thought fraud on the scale that existed at Enron was possible. Employees were aggressively encouraged by Enron's leaders to keep their 401K monies in Enron stock. Many did and suffered massive losses.[3]

People near retirement are losing their jobs and find it difficult, if not impossible, to find replacement positions with comparable incomes or social standing. This comes at a time when there is supposed to be a war for talent. There are thousands of jobs advertised on the Internet, but people apply and never hear about the disposition of their application. Some people have been outsourced, downsized, and otherwise let go three or four times and are confused about why this keeps happening. They have no choice, or so it seems, but to again try to find an employer who is worth being loyal to—one who will be loyal to them.

Since 9/11, the world is closer to America than we ever thought possible. The oceans off America's shores and friendly neighbors north and south no longer protect. Vigilante groups are actively patrolling our borders with Mexico and Canada in an effort to keep the "visigoths" at bay. The blame game is in full force. Some people blame the North American Free Trade Agreement (NAFTA) for shipping "our" jobs to Mexico. Others argue it is greedy corporations whose only allegiance is to increased profitability, and who will do anything, including destroying the American middle class, to get it.

As people lose their jobs, they also risk losing accessibility to affordable health care insurance. It is in vogue to blame the American Medical Association (AMA) for this because they have been the most effective and persistent advocate for the current system. Historically, the AMA has resisted any attempt to institute a national system of health coverage. Of course, liberals and conservatives blame each other. Since some of the best heart surgeons, for example, are in India and offer their services at a tenth of the cost of American doctors, some have even taken to blaming them.

The confusion will undoubtedly inspire public debate and eventually changes in public policy. But individuals are not in a position to wait for change to happen. Their careers and transitions hang in the balance, and relying on favorable public policy outcomes is risky business.

When futurists are done identifying the megatrends of our time, we are left with a definitive lack of clarity about the implications these trends have for individuals and what they should/can do about them. For example, we are being told that our jobs are moving to places in the world where they can be done more cheaply and that the need to find more efficient modes of production is being driven by consumer demand. Companies that cannot keep up will cease to exist. Should Americans worry about this? While the answers are mixed, there is universal agreement there will be disruptions in the workforce. In the short run, some of us will be negatively impacted by these disruptions while others will survive and prosper. People want to know how to get on the side of survival and prosperity. They want to know whether they personally can survive the storm—whether they can find safe havens in which to have careers. But when they turn to look for answers, they are confronted with a career management industry whose tools were developed largely in the 1970s. These tools focus on things like résumé writing, interviewing, and career management, but not on things dealing with global trends and how they impact an individual's employability.

Literature supporting the career management industry is largely of the how-to variety. The link that is missing connects the macro trends with strategies that individuals can use to manage their current reality. It involves more than tools; it requires a shift in mind-set of substantial proportions. Only then can individuals begin to imagine what to do in a world in which the kinds of jobs for which they have prepared may not exist now or ever again.

ECONOMY IN TRANSITION: EXPANSION, CONTRACTION, AND GLOBALIZATION

This shift in mind-set is better understood against the backdrop of the transitions the American economy has gone through since World War II, transitions that took place in the context of a global economy.

There have been three major transitions since that war: expansion, contraction, and globalization. None has been a one-way street. That is, movement from one to another is often an ebb-and-flow, making it difficult at any one point in time to tell exactly where a company is along the continuum. Additionally, the phases are not exclusive of one another. Numerous examples of efficiency-driven contraction can be found even though we may be firmly into globalization. This is true for entire industries as well as individual companies. In 2005, General Motors announced its intention to go global with major infrastructure investments in Europe and Asia at a time when it was laying off thousands of workers elsewhere. IBM's announcement in 2004 that it would add an estimated 15,000 employees (postwar expansion) was not inconsistent with most of the hires being outside the United States (globalization).

The third transition phase is well under way and promises to create more turmoil and opportunity than the other two combined. But all three have major consequences, sometimes for the nation and at other times for the entire world—but at all times for individual employees and their families. At one level these transitions greatly influence which and how many employees companies wish to hire and retain. At another, they influence what individuals need to do to make themselves employable.

In a fundamental sense, this is a book about change and how individuals and institutions adjust. It is about why corporate promises of employment for life have morphed into a greater likelihood of being downsized, outsourced, or let go. It is about the millions of people who have been laid off, anticipate being laid off, or know of someone looking for work. It is about the insecurity any of us feel about our jobs, careers, and retirement prospects as well as the ways in which companies adjust in response to market pressures for greater efficiencies.

This is not a "how-to" book, though there is a smidgen of that. Rather, it is a book about "why so"—why you will probably have to look for a new job sometime during your career and perhaps a new career sometime during the course of your life. It is a book written in response to the confusion people feel about what is happening to them as employees and what they can and should do about it. If individuals understand what is happening in the world of work today, they have a better chance of developing and implementing personal plans with improved chances of success.

Losing one's job is an emotional experience that shocks the system, even though one might have seen it coming. One way to help people deal with and prepare for this experience is to put it in a larger context. That way, not only does one come to understand they are not alone (i.e., a lot of people lose their jobs these days), but just maybe they can see themselves as being more in charge than ever before. Even if the forces of change are bigger than we are, it does not mean that we are unable to exert some measure of control.

This book is written largely from the perspective of the individual, but also includes a robust discussion about the forces governing corporate behavior. The motivations behind the behavior of corporations provide the context in which individuals seek employment opportunities.

We intuitively seem to understand why corporations need blueprints (strategic plans) for managing in a competitive environment. It makes sense that these plans are used to concentrate scarce resources (mainly time and money) to complete an organization's assigned tasks. What may not be as clear is that these blueprints invariably contain significant implications for individual employees. For example, after World War II there was a rapid expansion of the American economy along with a corresponding expansion of the need for a new kind of white-collar, professional worker. To attract these workers, companies expanded employee benefits, career opportunities, and pension programs. The corresponding blueprint adjustment made by individuals was to concentrate their time and resources by going to college to get in line for the good jobs, and Americans went to college in unprecedented numbers.[4]

By 1960, white-collar workers outnumbered their blue-collar counterparts for the first time and by 1990 had become a full majority of the workforce.[5] White-collar work is now what most of us do; and by looking at the most

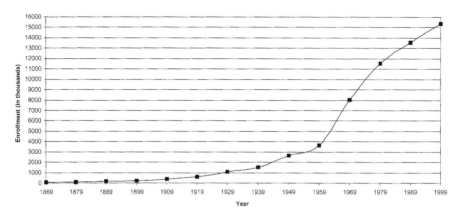

Figure 1.1 College enrollment by decade, 1869–1999.
Source: DoE, 1996.

recent past of the white-collar worker, we can see an outline of our most immediate future.

For example, as the postwar expansion leveled off, many American-based companies adjusted their methods of operation to produce goods and services more efficiently. Those that did survived (GE, IBM, and Exxon), and those that did not failed (Bendix, Collins Radio, and Curtiss-Wright). In many instances the adjustments called for smaller workforces. Consequently, what was once seen as winning the war for talent was later looked upon as unnecessary hiring and the creation of bloated staffs.

Americans, especially white-collar workers, were unaccustomed to being laid off. And even after layoffs became commonplace, the very best companies— those viewed as offering good jobs, such as IBM—had no layoff policies in place. But many of these policies were not sustainable and were eventually abandoned. The new blueprint for corporate America gave rise to a corresponding set of adjustments by individual employees who needed to manage their transitions from one company to another. In response, an entire industry, outplacement, emerged. Before 1970, outplacement firms by and large did not exist. By 1980 there were fifty. By 1988 there were more than 200 firms, complete with an industry association and an association of professionals.[6] The notion of employment for life no longer characterized the American lifestyle. The constant restructuring of the workplace to control the cost of labor replaced it. And restructuring became the accepted way of doing business not only in America, but in Japan, Europe, Mexico, China, and anywhere companies participated in the global economy.

It now appears that the economic recovery of the first decade of this millennium may be the first jobless recovery in American history; that is, economic growth and increases in productivity are not associated with the creation of new jobs. Advances in technology are eliminating jobs not just in America but in

China, India, and all over the globe. Job elimination through technology and outsourcing is alive and well.

William Bridges offered a persuasive take on this in his book *Job Shift*. He observed that companies are rethinking the way work gets done by "dejobbing" their organizations.[7] Among other things, they are organizing workers into self-managed teams. In this sense, no one individual has a set of activities that constitutes "their" job. Instead, activities shift among members of a team until the desired results are achieved. This allows for flatter, more efficient organizations with less managerial infrastructure. So jobs with titles of supervisor, manager, and director are giving way to "dejobbed" teams without the currently ubiquitous job descriptions.

Finally, Frances Cairncross (*The Death of Distance*) reported that our work today involves managing data more than things. And data can be managed anywhere in the world. This "death of distance" has loosened the grip of geography, and "people, some at least, will gain more freedom to live far from their employers. Some kinds of work will be organized in three shifts, to maximize the use of the world's three main time zones: the Americas, East Asia, Australia, and Europe. Time zones and language groups, rather than mileage, will come to define distance."[8]

The postwar contraction, along with white-collar jobs becoming fungible across national boundaries, gave rise to two new categories of white-collar workers—the "unemployed" and the "anxiously employed," according to Barbara Ehrenreich in her book *Bait and Switch*. Members of the first group are perhaps familiar to many of us because of the frequency of mergers, acquisitions, and restructurings resulting in white- collar workers being laid off. The second group may be less familiar. As Ehrenreich noted:

> The Bureau of Labor Statistics measures under-employment only in terms of one's hours; that is, you are officially under-employed only if you are working part-time and would prefer to work full-time. In March of 2004, the unemployment rate was 5.8 percent while the under-employment rate, measured strictly as involuntary part-time work, was 10 percent. As to the proportion of people employed at low-paying jobs that make no use of their education or established skill sets, no reliable estimates are available. I found plenty of people though who had gone from unemployment to under-employment in the sense of having to work at jobs inappropriate to their skills.[9]

There is anecdotal evidence to suggest that the numbers of those anxiously employed are greater than we could imagine. Many of them work for Manpower, or Adecco (a temporary employment agency headquartered in the Netherlands and even larger than Manpower), or are self-employed as independent contractors with companies such as Mary Kay, AFLAC, or anyone of a number of others. They show up in the Bureau of Labor Statistics data as employed, even though in positions without many of the attributes we have come to associate with good jobs—or at least jobs befitting their education, skills, and experience. Many of these are jobs without company-paid pensions and/or health care benefits. Long-term employment is neither anticipated nor necessarily encouraged, and career development is little more than advertising designed to induce greater sales levels. Workers are getting by on less income than they ever thought possible.

For many, their value in the marketplace has been diminished as if by some unknown force. And the concern is that this will be the fate of many more to come, as an entire generation prepares for jobs that either may later not exist or are best done elsewhere. If so, we may be entering a time of downward mobility few want and even fewer expect. For those losing their jobs, health care coverage, retirement pensions, and the ability to send their children to college, the American dream is becoming the American nightmare. At one level these are subjects for public policy inspired by great visions—the kind provided by FDR (the New Deal), Kennedy (space travel), and Reagan (the Berlin Wall). At another level though, each person—those in or concerned about being in transition as well as those engaged in career planning—want to know: Are there any good jobs left?

Megatrends shape what companies need to do to be competitive. In a global economy that means being responsive to customer demands for customization, quality, and price in creative ways. The way companies behave in turn shapes what individuals need to do to become eligible for the jobs companies offer. These linkages define major patterns in our lives and are the grounds on which we compete for our individual pieces of the economic pie. Understanding and mastering these linkages will require unparalleled levels of personal career literacy, which can be developed more easily if one understands that they exist as well as how they work. That is the journey on which we are about to embark. Nothing less than survival and prosperity are at stake.

CHAPTER TWO

❧✦

ABOUT YOU, ME, AND ROY

- Me
- My two grown sons
- Both of my sisters
- My brother
- Both of my brothers-in-law
- My closest friend and his wife
- All seven of my direct reports
- Four of my last six bosses
- The president of my former company
- The CEO of my former company and the past four CEOs I have worked with
- Well-known people we read and hear about every day, and
- Roy

This list is a reality check to make sure I keep from exaggerating just how many people I know or hear about who at one time were between jobs. To me, it seems like the numbers have grown to where practically everyone you meet has at some point lost their job, anticipates losing it, or knows of someone who has. Perhaps I am naive, but these people appear to be productive and many are very talented. We asked earlier: When did workers become so disposable? The follow-on question is: What can be done about it?

These questions are of some urgency because of the warp speed at which the world about us is changing. It is amusing to read about the late-nineteenth-century proposal to close the United States Bureau of Patents because, in the words of one of its proponents, "everything worth inventing has just about been invented." Today change happens so quickly we hardly have time to react, let alone understand. Yet for each of us there is a sense that the personal stakes continue to escalate.

Over the past several years I have spoken to hundreds of college students who are anxious about their prospects in the job market. Their anxiety is different from what their parents experienced in that it is a concern about whether jobs they are preparing for will exist long enough for them to have a career. Their concerns are well founded.

The availability of jobs will ebb and flow depending on forces in the marketplace, including technology and concerns about efficiency. When companies are free to move jobs to their most rational economic locations, those who held those jobs become part of the labor pool in need of redeployment. For the economist, workforce redeployment is looked upon as an engine for economic development as workers migrate to other jobs and companies reinvest to get better returns on capital. For individual workers, redeployment can be a source of economic demise because their jobs move elsewhere or disappear altogether. There is no benign mechanism that redeploys workers on an as-needed basis. Instead, people (especially Americans) are left to fend for themselves, and there is no assurance they will share in any of the economic benefits workforce redeployment generates for society as a whole. In this sense, workers become disposable. The difference between now and an earlier time is that back then, redeployment happened over long periods of time. The movement of the farming population to urban centers is an example of a redeployment that took well over a century. We are now down to one or two decades and getting shorter.

There was a time when our careers or occupational choices were prescribed by what our fathers did. Sons of farmers became farmers and their daughters became farmers' wives. Later, greater access to education gave men, and then women, access to jobs unavailable to their fathers a generation earlier. Still later it became common for people to have several jobs during the course of a career and more than one career in the course of a lifetime. But freedom has been both a source of liberation as well as confinement.

The idea of having a choice about careers is a relatively recent phenomenon and became possible only when survival was no longer an issue for daily resolution. Then, as people moved from an ascribed status in life to one that was attained, being free to make career choices became more real. But it is a freedom bringing an unprecedented set of anxieties and insecurities. In this context, personal freedom and security can be at odds with one another.

If ever there was a golden age for both freedom and security, it existed in post–World War II America for the burgeoning white-collar workforce, as described in Chapter One. These were new jobs for a new generation, with promises of a lifetime of career advancement and pension support in retirement—all with the same employer.

While it has never been quite this cut-and-dried, it does seem fair to say that whatever post–World War II job security existed has given way to a more complicated reality. The expectation today is that we will be free (forced) to change both jobs and careers. Consequently, we are facing levels of complexity unknown just a few generations ago. At the same time, what we do for a living (and whom we do it for) continues to play an important role in our self-esteem. Our occupational choices feed our egos and affect how others view us.

Bill Russell, the great basketball player for the Boston Celtics, was often taken aback by this blending of occupation and ego. Being six-foot-ten, he was accustomed to strangers asking, "Are you a basketball player?" His response often was, "Basketball is what I do, it is not who I am." Mr. Russell understood the difference between his occupation and his central being. Russell's objections notwithstanding, our work *is* important and influences our sense of who we are as well as our social status.

But if having a job of which we are proud is important, losing that job can be devastating. Being let go/fired is often viewed as a threat to our sense of personal worth and value, as it tends to invalidate everything we know and believe about ourselves. "I was laid off," the reasoning goes, "so what I thought about myself is not true. My personal effectiveness with people—the value I bring to my organization and my peers and the esteem with which I am held in the community—must be less than I thought or they would have laid off somebody else." These insecurities and anxieties are the other side of workforce redeployment and why being let go feels a lot more personal than it actually is. And, as it turns out, finding the right replacement job is trickier today than ever before, adding complexity to the lives of so many people.

"I'M BETWEEN JOBS"

I meet and engage new people in conversations almost every working day. Sometimes these conversations take place in the course of my work with people who are in transition. Just as often, however, they take place when traveling, and consequently I come in contact with people from all walks of life. They start with the usual pleasantries but quickly get around to what they do for a living. The answers vary, but the patterns of the conversations vary less.

It is fairly common for people to acknowledge, "Right now, I am between jobs." That so many people share this experience is surprising. That it is now so easily the subject of "polite" conversation is absolutely startling. There is a general sense among the people I meet that "American" jobs are disappearing. Quotation marks are used here because I'm concerned that some people may believe that jobs done by Americans inherently belong to people here, and if they go elsewhere it is a threat to our national security. Now might be a good time for Americans, and the rest of the world, to get familiar with the debate regarding globalization. Other countries will later make these same arguments even more forcibly as their jobs migrate toward cheaper labor pools.

There is a role for government, but there is some question about government's ability to contain jobs within national boundaries. Since data can be shipped, stored, manipulated, and managed from almost anywhere in the world, it is more easily transported across national boundaries and not easy to regulate. For now, there seems to have been a sea change in what Americans are experiencing relative to their jobs and careers.

The number of people who have lost their jobs is so large it numbs the mind, and most have no way of comprehending the size of the issue. Another way of looking at the 43 million people laid off between 1979 and 1995 is to think of it as 10,300 Americans losing their jobs each day of a five-day workweek for the entire sixteen-year period. According to some, we have entered the age of "Jack Welch" economics. Welch, former CEO of General Electric (GE), is credited with eliminating over 100,000 jobs, and by so doing boosted shareholder returns there to historic levels. By one estimate Welch increased GE's market capitalization by more than $450 billion and "established himself as (one of) the most admired business leaders in the world." Laying people off can be difficult, especially when layoffs are not a part of the social fabric of the way business is done. Welch himself felt that and observed:

> Unfortunately, in the 1980s most of GE's employment levels were headed downward. We went from 411,000 employees at the end of 1980 to 299,000 by the end of 1985. Of the 112,000 people who left the GE payroll, about 37,000 were in businesses we sold, but 81,000 people—or 1 in every 5 in our business—lost their jobs for productivity reasons.
>
> From the numbers, you could make the case that there was either a Neutron Jack or a company with too many positions. I naturally took comfort in the latter, but the Neutron tag still got me down.[1]

Welch's message is: Making General Electric stronger by making it more efficient was the right thing to do. Most corporate executives undoubtedly now believe we have entered an age in which it is the only thing to do if a company is to survive. Layoffs have become an acceptable and expected way of doing business. In addition, any notion that the CEO has a familial responsibility to his community has also all but disappeared. While one cannot be sure it ever existed, today's executives (American executives in particular) are not known for imposing pain and suffering on themselves as they force employees to bear the brunt of workforce restructurings. In this sense chivalry is dead, and along with it is any notion that the corporation represents a community of interests akin to that of the nation itself. In the long run this may come to be viewed as the sacrifice of an incredibly valuable asset.

Being outsourced, downsized, and let go is replacing its predecessor of employment for life, company-sponsored career development, and company-paid pensions. The more cynical view is that company-paid transition support for terminated employees was little more than "blood money" that helped ease the conscience of corporate executives. These monies also gave rise to the career transition industry and its job-finding methodologies. The help this industry offers covers a wide variety of subjects, including how to:

- Write a résumé
- Network

- Approach the job market
- Get the first interview
- Relocate your family
- Relocate without really relocating
- Use the Internet to find a job
- Start a business
- Write a business plan
- Use search firms
- Negotiate job offers, and
- Many, many more

Help managing the traditional components of the career transition process is available. However, our focus is on the megatrends and how people need to integrate them into their personal situations. To do this, I will introduce you to some people who have been let go and are participants in an actual networking group run by an outplacement firm. The purpose is to provide the reader with an up close and personal look at how the process works and why it needs to change.

You will meet people who made large mistakes as they worked through losing and then finding new opportunities. Others managed the process with relative ease. Many were frightened, others supremely confident. All, however, were able to get through the transitions of job loss and/or career change without permanent damage to their psyches. But the differences in their experiences resulted more from their respective levels of understanding rather than differences in skill sets.

You will read about people trying to write reasonably attractive résumés in the face of major gaps in their employment history. There is a divorced mother of three who discovers her formula for career success. There is also an entrepreneur who wants to be his own boss, but initially for all the wrong reasons. These are the stories of real people who have successfully managed their situations and personal circumstances. Their experiences provide insight into how one might integrate knowledge about today's marketplace of jobs and careers into their respective realities.

Seeing *what* people do is only half the equation. We also need to focus on *why*. Toward that end, you will also come to understand more precisely how we got to this point where job eliminations and layoffs make heroes rather than villains of CEOs. Later you will also read about the multiplier role that technology has played in this process. While improvements in technology make it possible to perform jobs anywhere in the world, it is globalization however that makes it imperative.

QUESTIONS TO CONSIDER

Some analysts argue that we are seeing the "McJobbing" of America, in which the great middle class is threatened because their jobs are being moved to

India, China, and Latin America. Soon all that will be left are jobs at the extremes of the pay spectrum, with nothing of substance in between.[2]

As we explore these issues, certain questions emerge. Do the rules by which we manage our careers change? Is it enough now to do well in high school, get into a good college, and land a job with the company of one's dreams? What else does one need to understand and act upon?

In the context of our brave new world, is it acceptable to lie on one's résumé? What is the difference between liberal embellishment and an outright lie? Is either acceptable, and how does one stay on the proper side of the truth? How does one manage gaps in their employment history? Is it fair that employers hold employment gaps against applicants for employment when workforce restructuring is one of the primary tools they use to manage their business? Practically anyone who is out of work, by definition, has a gap in their employment history. How should that be managed? Once one lands a position, should they quit looking for another one? What happens if one accepts a job and their "dream job" opens shortly thereafter? The answers to these and other questions are influenced by the realities of today's job marketplace. Questions such as these are intended to get behind the data and look directly into the faces and hearts of people who are "between jobs" and perhaps struggling mightily with the hands they have been dealt and the questions before them. This opportunity can provide the reader with an informed realism as well as an understanding of job marketplace dynamics. The college graduate needs to know that some companies are promising long-term careers while terminating the employment of thousands of others. How can the two be reconciled? Should such companies be avoided?

It is helpful to understand that finding the right job or career is not a linear process. There are ups, downs, and moves sideways. Sometimes there are little steps forward accompanied by giant steps backward. These are further complicated when unanticipated things happen for no apparent reason at all.

Understanding the context in which we live and work has yet another advantage. Perhaps you recall the *Alice in Wonderland* scene in which Alice is running about frantically asking the Cheshire Cat which of the many doors available she should enter. "That," replies the Cat, "depends on where you are going."

"I don't know where I am going," says Alice.

"Then, which door doesn't really matter."

The high anxiety that comes with losing and then finding work or launching a new career can put us in an *Alice in Wonderland*–type frenzy. Several of the doors may appear to lead to good companies with good jobs, but should they be taken? That depends on where we see ourselves going and for what we might be looking. I continue to meet people who have been downsized three and four times over relatively short periods of time. Does that mean they took the wrong jobs? Some of them are well positioned to do other things immediately. Others (a clear majority) are both surprised and displeased with this unfortunate turn of events. To them the search for another good job ended in a blind alley. More times than not, those who are disappointed misunderstand the world of work and the new employee value propositions being offered in the marketplace today.

THE EMPLOYMENT VALUE PROPOSITION

The term "employment value proposition" means the promises an employer makes to employees in exchange for their loyalty. Though often explicit, the proposition is sometimes implied, making clarity difficult. In these instances, employers can more easily work conflicting sides of the street; giving the appearance of offering traditional good jobs while simultaneously being free to restructure and accommodate their economic interests at will.

This statement should not be taken in any way to imply that companies purposively deceive. Some do, but most do not. Take note of the way in which the people you will meet in the following chapters are engaged in the transition process. They all use résumés and interviewing techniques to show each potential employer their side of the employment value proposition. In this sense, they seek to be understood in the context of the value they bring to the table. The most successful among them, however, will be those who themselves understand as well as those who are understood.

In January 2005, in *The New York Times Book Review*, there was a discussion of the perennially best-selling career guide *What Color Is Your Parachute?* The reviewer observed, "Parachute arrived on the scene [thirty-five years ago] when business practices and employee ideals and attitudes were beginning to shift. The postwar loyalty ethic, in which workers got security in exchange for obedience, was dying."[3]

Attitudes on both sides (employer and employee) were changing in concert with one another. My own personal observation is that there has been a substantial and critically important lag on the part of both employers and employees alike. Many employers are still using the language of long-term employment, company-sponsored career development, and pension benefits as key components of their recruiting value proposition. Yet their behavior in the marketplace, as dictated by the competitive environment, follows patterns of downsizing and outsourcing. The applicant who focuses only on convincing the employer of the value they bring to the equation will likely miss seeing the larger context in which companies operate. They will tend to view future adjustments to their benefits, pensions, and career development opportunities as yet other examples of greedy corporations. The employee who understands how corporations work and how they survive in the face of changing economic circumstances stands a much better chance of surviving through to prosperity.

Today people are more sophisticated and realistic about the boundary lines between them and their employers. They are probably becoming less loyal in the sense of viewing both sides of the employment value proposition more completely. In this context, it is better to understand and anticipate. It is important to know that while many companies prefer to hire employees who have a long-term horizon for their working tenure with them, they often are not in a position to guarantee long-term employment. Mergers, divestitures, restructurings, and general business conditions sometimes get in the way.

Companies generally do not recruit prospective employees with the intent of reneging. But I have seen far too many cases in which people have been hired or relocated only to face job elimination within a few months of starting. I continue to encounter far too many people who changed companies, moved their families, and are out of work shortly thereafter.

Recent studies by Hewitt Associates, the Conference Board, DDI, and others report declining levels of employee commitment to their jobs and employers. They are less loyal, committed, and engaged because they perceive that to be the environment in which they work. Their employers are that way.

During the job recruiting process, people will likely hear many implied promises about the future. Certainly companies are highly invested in their recruiting processes, and their futures rely heavily on attracting and retaining the right employees for the right periods of time. There are times and circumstances, however, when they will not (and cannot) live up to the commitments they make, implied or otherwise. In these instances the consequences fall most immediately and heavily on the individual rather than on the organization they joined. In today's environment it is far wiser to understand both sides of the employment value proposition. But *Are There Any Good Jobs Left?* is not about companies and their search for engaged employees. Rather, it is aimed at the other end of the spectrum. It is a book about the survival and success of the individual. It is a book about you, me and . . .

ROY

Roy, my father-in-law, had an admirable set of life experiences. He was an Eagle Scout, the only one of three children to attend college, a U.S. Navy pilot during World War II, and a designer and builder of semi-tractor trailer trucks. His last assignment was in Northern California, where he led the design team that built an assembly plant, and then he ran the facility as its general manager. In the early years of my marriage to his daughter, I was on the faculty at the University of California, Riverside. During our many fishing excursions for Pacific salmon in the early 1970s, I would seek Roy's advice about making a career change from education to business. That series of conversations was the start of a thirty-year exchange of ideas about business and its changing landscape. The conversations paralleled the massive changes taking place in the work environment and demonstrated our misreading of the situation. Roy's thought process helped him figure out how he should manage his own career.

The conclusions he drew were directly linked to his read of the situation. Further, the price he paid seemed in direct proportion to the variation of his conclusions from the realities of what was actually happening. It is a price extracted from any of us when our view of the world is at variance with reality. The difference between now and then is that things are happening on such a massive scale and at such a rapid pace, the price one pays for misunderstanding has risen.

It is helpful to know that Roy started his business career in 1945, and I started mine thirty years later. Neither of us was born into families with professional business backgrounds. Consequently, most of what we learned came from firsthand (and first time) experiences. We did not have much of a sense of business history or theory, nor did we know whether what we were learning were long-term tried-and-true methods of doing business or if they were relatively new. As it turned out, what Roy saw, experienced, and acted upon was heavily influenced by World War II and its immediate aftermath. In contrast, my business reality was one in which postwar policies and organizational structures were beginning to adjust to new realities. The conversations Roy and I had and our respective frames of reference have relevancy for understanding our world today.

MANAGING EXCESS WORKERS

Shortly after making a transition to a *Fortune* 100 firm, I recall being summoned to a meeting with the CEO along with several others. Attendance did not follow organizational lines but instead was based on "the need to know." As one of the most junior and least experienced of the attendees, I had no idea how unsettling this was to the four layers of those between me and the CEO who were not invited. As I had no frame of reference, I did not know if having such meetings was unusual or not. I learned later that this was not the way post–World War II hierarchies functioned.

The chairman spoke first, advising us that we were here to work on two special projects designed to help boost the price of our stock and improve shareholder confidence. He then turned the meeting over to the chief financial officer, who explained that the market had gone soft, our cost of production (mainly fuel costs) was going through the roof, and share price was taking a hit. All of this was hurting our ability to raise capital for acquisitions.

Two programs were to be announced simultaneously. The first was a reduction in force (RIF), in which there would be an across-the-board head count cut of 10 percent. Our job was to make sure the right people got released, that all company divisions and departments did their fair share, and that there were programs in place to help people transition to employment opportunities outside the company. These ideas were new to me, but I had no reason to suspect they were also relatively new to business as well. The second program had to do with employee assistance. When I first heard these words,

I remember saying to myself, "What are we going to assist employees in doing?" I soon found out. The program's newly appointed director began his presentation by announcing that he was a recovering alcoholic. Even during his lowest moments he was able to hide his dependence on alcohol from most of his fellow workers, but he never was as productive as he needed to be.

"As the pressures on our profit margins continue, employee productivity is being scrutinized more closely," he said. He then presented a dizzying array of statistics that showed estimated productivity losses because of alcoholism and drug abuse in the workplace. This new program would train managers to spot substance abusers, get them into recovery programs, or terminate them if they refused or did not improve.

The following summer I continued a conversation with Roy that had started a few years earlier. It was about a member of his staff who was dealing with alcoholism. He had gotten beyond the stage of being able to hide his dysfunction and had been in and out of company-sponsored rehabilitation programs. His situation was becoming increasingly critical from a health perspective. Plus, he had a stay-at-home wife and thirteen children. The company had been shuffling him from one department to another in an effort to minimize the impact of his lack of productivity. Over the years, Roy had handled similar employee situations the same way.

I walked Roy through our employee assistance program and how it tied to the performance appraisal system. Roy listened but did not appear impressed enough to try this approach. Only retrospectively am I beginning to understand that conversation. I now see that we had different endgames. Roy's focus was on the thirteen children, in the context of social norms that encouraged moving nonproductive white-collar workers into less critical staff jobs. I am not prepared to say he was wrong. Roy was dealing with one individual who was part of a relatively new white-collar group. It was one person in an unusual context, and hiding the occasional misfit was the socially responsible and appropriate thing to do. However, this was the end of one era and the beginning of another with regard to white-collar workers.

The situation I was in was altogether different, the beginning of the next era. My meetings had to do with productivity, stock price, fuel costs, and shareholder value. We were talking about what to do with large numbers of people in the context of megatrends.

As our plans were implemented and Wall Street responded positively, I was struck by thinking how each layoff must have a face behind it. The largeness of the process never fully masked the reality of its impact on people. I have often thought to myself, the important difference between the decision Roy had to make and the one my company made was in the faces of the people. Roy could see them and we could not. We knew most of the workers personally, but not all. We knew some of their families, but not most. So when Wall Street rewarded us with a boost in stock price, we quit being bothered by our inability to look into the faces and souls of our people.

Retrospectively, I am startled by how quickly the company seized permission to lay off its excess workers. There were several layers of supporting rationale. The business case came first. Stock price, bond rating, and access to capital at favorable rates required that action be taken. The people stuff came next. By taking these actions, the company maintained its economic health and preserved jobs for the great majority. Those who were to be let go would get transition assistance and should be able, according to statistics, to find other good jobs shortly. In short, the RIF was a "win-win" for all concerned.

I remember it was shortly thereafter that I did my first "pay for performance" study, which reinforced the company's focus on employee productivity. We gathered data and ran correlations (regression analyses) on variations in the sizes of merit increases. The findings stunned me then, but not now. Men in management positions with children in college tended to get larger merit increases than others. This was irrespective of income level or performance rating. The idea that some men got raises more as a function of their perceived financial need as heads of households rather than for their contribution to the business seems strange in today's context. It was not strange that there were no women in the study and that the men were all white.

I did not quite know what to make of all of this then. It is clearer now. The "efficiency" rationale used by the company must have seemed strange to those being laid off. They undoubtedly thought of themselves as normally productive employees with good records. Such people had never in the company's history lost their jobs. The conversation around the watercooler largely attributed the RIF to the new CEO's need to put his stamp on things. Regardless, this was a different way of doing business—one that would accelerate and eventually come to dominate corporate life for years to come.

EARLY RETIREMENT

The next exchange with Roy came during one of those typical weekend family telephone calls you make just to catch up and stay in touch. It was then that Roy announced he had made a decision to retire and move to Moss Beach. He and his wife anticipated supporting themselves by becoming real estate agents in the area. I didn't know if the idea made any sense. However, I did know that Roy was not an impulsive person, and selling real estate at this stage in life was just about as reasonable as anything else. But he did not seem to me to be the typical real estate type. As it turned out he wasn't, and the new career was relatively short-lived as he shortly thereafter retired permanently to San Diego.

Over the course of the next few years, Roy and I would have conversations about what prompted him to retire so abruptly. I had always been careful to avoid broaching the topic myself, because of obvious sensitivity. Over time, he volunteered bits and pieces. Roy's company was in the early stages of desperation, and like so many others was trying to control costs and improve margins. They had fully anticipated closing selected facilities, reducing head count, and dispersing key personnel to other locations. Roy fell into the latter category and was given an opportunity to move back east to the corporate headquarters and take a staff job with a director's title. The entire proposition amounted to a fistful of unattractive options. Moving away from California, taking a staff job, and losing his vice president's title were just too much to take. He was able to work out a deal whereby he got extended severance payments, continued health care coverage, and a pension sweetener if he wanted to retire.

Fortunately, Roy had always been financially prudent and was in a position to retire without serious sacrifice to his standard of living. However, the money was not the point. A lot of the good feeling Roy had about himself was tied up with being an automotive engineer and vice president of a respected company. He not only had a good job, he had one of the very best available. Having to retire in his early sixties meant there were not very many good jobs left, at least not by Roy's definition. As he became more comfortable with being retired, he returned to graduate school to study astronomy. By today's standards he cut a pretty good deal. Still, he was not entirely happy because retirement at this time was not the value proposition he had signed up for. Nor was it what had kept him there all these years. He really liked being the plant's general manager. He was well known and respected in the community, and this was not the graceful end to his career he had anticipated. What appeared to be an awkward move by Roy's company at an awkward time, in retrospect, was a career interrupted by the demands of global competition. It was an interruption that would grow and threaten to consume him, me, and perhaps all of us.

LOYALTY TAKES A FINAL BLOW

Later we were in San Diego, and I was trying to figure out how I might approach the subject that I was changing jobs, yet again, and relocating the family. For me this happened about every three or four years, and I was feeling a slight twinge of discomfort about it. Sometimes I moved on because it seemed like the thing to do. At other times I had no choice. My so-called career began to look like a series of random events rather than the result of a disciplined thought process. Thank goodness my new jobs were always bigger and better than the ones before. But this still was especially hard for me to explain to Roy. Loyalty was such a core component of who he was and how he conducted his business. In contrast, my job-hopping had almost no loyalty associated with it at all. By then I noticed that employers were beginning to actively seek out candidates who had experience working in more than one or two organizations. They wanted people who they thought could adjust quickly and work in a variety of settings. Quite accidentally, my job-hopping became an asset rather than a liability. It was in this context that Roy and I had our final conversation about the changing world of work. Just as I was about to announce my newest job change, Roy said, "I wish I had been able to change jobs like you." I was, of course, surprised. It was then I learned of a job offer he got a few years before retiring. It was from a rapidly growing bus company that wanted him to design, build, and run an assembly plant in Northern California. The money was better and the pension was guaranteed. He turned it down without a serious review because of loyalty to his own company and a belief in what they had been able to build together.

My sense, then as now, was that his decision to stay is probably the one that most of us would have made, especially back then. Who knew that the organizational paradigms implemented in response to World War II were under siege? Who could tell that the world was about to change so dramatically? The only question is: What can and should we do about it? In light of what is happening, what decisions does one need to make about paying for health care, their children's education, and retirement? What will happen to those things, and how will we survive this age of disposable workers?

Over the course of the next few chapters, you will meet individual members of a networking group whose companies have hired an outplacement firm to help them transition to new employment. You will see them, on a personal level, deal with a wide range of issues associated with looking for jobs and managing careers. They will share their feelings with you. These are feelings we all may have but are sometimes unwilling or unable to share with each other, or admit to ourselves.

"I am embarrassed about being fired."

"Companies will think I can't hold a job."

"Maybe I should start my own business."

"It's a great job, but I don't want to relocate my family ... again."

"Why can't I just post my résumé on the Internet and wait?"

"I can't believe it. I just moved here and they've eliminated my job already."

"Employers are not as loyal as they used to be."

The reader should know that while all the people included here are real, they represent a composite of people that I and my colleagues have met while working in the career transition business. I have chosen to emphasize getting people to ask the right questions—inquiries whose answers will provide the greatest advantage to individuals as they plan their careers or next job moves. As you read about members of the networking group dealing with their situations, I encourage you to think about the flow of their logic and the consequences of the kinds of questions they choose to ask. As one improves the quality of their questions, I assure you that they will also improve the quality of the answers they get.

CHAPTER THREE

HOW DID WE GET HERE FROM THERE?

WE ARE ABOUT to look in on the start of a networking group made up of people in transition and facilitated by a career transition professional. It is a group that could not have existed fifty years ago. What they are experiencing and the patterns of their thought are the result of their current situations. Such groups will continue to exist and grow in number. Their collective thinking will also evolve quickly over the coming decade as their circumstances become more familiar to larger numbers of people worldwide.

The kinds of questions they ask are the same ones that will need to be asked by those who are currently gainfully employed as well as by those just entering the workforce. Unfortunately, many ask these questions only when they absolutely have to—that is, when looking for a job. There is a great advantage in knowing the answers ahead of time.

THE GROUP

Eight people, seven of whom are strangers to one another, are gathered in a single room. The space they occupy and how it is appointed places this gathering in practically any city in North America. In truth, it could be in almost any city anywhere in the world. The lighting and sound acoustics are understated, inviting a sort of mature quietness so typical of business decorum in large and small companies alike. Very soon people will introduce themselves and begin a journey together that will change all of their tomorrows. Few recognize the important nature of this gathering. Most do not even want to be there. So far, the only person they know in common is the person who will facilitate the group and who has urged them to attend against, if not their better judgment, at least their wishes. But these views are not held so strongly as to invite rebellion. They are here waiting for the meeting to begin. Meanwhile, a subdued tension settles over the room just as it does when any group of strangers comes together for the first time.

Some of the more outgoing types have started to introduce themselves, and a muffled undercurrent of conversations half fills the room. "Hi, I'm Bob Watson," one of the conversations begins, "until recently, I was with..." While these people do not know one another's backgrounds, family situations, or attitudes, each knows they have at least one thing in common. They have all recently been terminated by their employer and are coming together to form a networking group as they begin the process of transitioning to the next stage of their lives. The company each one used to work for has hired an outplacement firm to make sure their transition to other employment goes as smoothly as possible. This "act of kindness" is actually a shrewd recognition of the need that companies have to protect their brand in the marketplace by treating departing employees well. Many companies, especially large ones such as GE, Ford, and GM, find themselves terminating one set of workers at the same time they are recruiting others. This apparent paradox has long ago passed into the realm of what we expect from corporations. At one time the idea of hiring and terminating people concurrently, many with similar qualifications, would numb our senses. Today companies are content with protecting their brand images simply by helping terminated employees transition. It helps their recruiting process.

Some members of the soon-to-be-formed group are unsure if they either need or want help. But they suspect that finding a job will not be easy because large layoffs are more common these days and a lot of people are out of work. They have all heard the horror stories of newspaper ads and Internet postings bringing hundreds, if not thousands, of résumé responses. Over the past few years most of them have noticed having met more and more people who have either lost their own job or know of someone who has. Beyond this vague sense of a link between general economic conditions and their individual situations, most are unsure how they got themselves in this predicament or exactly what to do to get out of it.

Most of the seven are thinking, "Why is this happening to me? They let the wrong person go." There is also a slight twinge of embarrassment for some because they have never had to look for work before. Instead, job offers always came looking for them. One member of the group has been with the same company his entire adult working life. For him, this gathering and the entire experience are overwhelming. All along, his plans were to retire early from his company and spend time traveling with his wife. Over the years this couple developed their own five-year plans. The first five years in retirement were to be spent visiting all the places they had hoped to see, but until now had neither the time nor money to. Understanding that five years' worth of travel without a break is impractical, they planned travel respites to visit their children and their families. And now—a few years away from being able to afford retirement and still having to pay for college educations, this man is out of a job, slightly afraid of the future, and wondering, silently to himself, if he should share his anxiety with his wife. Little does he realize that very soon he will feel comfortable enough to share his concerns even with this group of strangers. He could also be angry if he only knew with whom to be angry.

A couple of people in the room have gone through this before, at least a few times. They know what this group is about and are prepared to offer their individual wisdom about how to navigate the whitewater rapids of looking for a job. Each time they found another good job and are reasonably confident of doing so again. Just beneath the confidence that comes with been there/done that lurks a number of insecurities. "I was younger when this happened before. Are companies hiring people my age?" The other veteran of the unemployment wars has been odd man out three times during his career and is worried that employers will think something is wrong with him. The first time it happened, he was part of a more general layoff because of a declining business climate. The second time was the result of a merger, even though he stayed on for six months in a consulting capacity. And now, he simply does not get along with his boss. It is a family business, and his boss's family members are the principal owners. This was an unfortunate turn of events because he went out of his way to choose an employer that had more of a family orientation—one that had good, old-fashioned values, where things were done with a handshake rather than through lawyers. These last two terminations happened in close proximity to one another time-wise, and he is worried that this will erode his reputation (brand) in the marketplace. The idea of thinking of oneself as having (or being) a brand is new. People are much like companies in that their reputations (brands) will play a significant role in how successful they will be in finding work.

There are a couple of women in the group. When this is the case, there is less behind-the-scenes whispering about reverse discrimination and how women get better breaks than men because they are protected by affirmative action and are not as quick to be fired. One woman has, up until now, had a real success story of a career. After a divorce and gaining custody of her three children, she opened her own advertising/marketing firm. There were a few years of sixty-hour workweeks before she landed a major account, ensuring the firm's survival and her own measure of economic independence. It was not long before her client offered her a position as executive vice president of marketing. She jumped at the chance. A year or so later the company was sold, and the acquirer had its own marketing executive who was asked to run the combined entity. Her credentials are impeccable, but she has no real experience looking for a job. That lack of experience is a source of anxiety.

During this time of small talk, another member of the group lets it be known that his severance agreement is such that he no longer needs to work. After six months of going to the gym, coaching little league, and playing golf, he is bored and wants to do something that has more meaning. However, the kind of position he wants is unclear.

You will meet some members of the group more thoroughly than others. For now, seven strangers are attending a meeting because their companies have hired a firm to help them with their transitions. The facilitator has met separately with each one and has suggested that they attend and begin networking. Never mind that most of them are unsure what networking is, especially in the context of a job search. All are competent professionals with years of positive job and life experiences. Yet all are slightly nervous. Their concerns are personal and can be difficult to discuss with others, especially strangers.

They are willing to give this first session a try because they have been encouraged to do so, and not because of any deeply held sense that it will help them. They trust the group's facilitator who, in private and in comforting detail, has pointed out that there are others who have the same questions and doubts they have. The facilitator is akin to a wilderness guide, who in a different setting would have to spend more time earning trust rather than having it bestowed. They have been advised that they are not alone and that terminating the employment of otherwise productive people is an increasingly common phenomenon the market will understand and accept, if they do likewise.

However, the facilitator's one-on-one sessions with group members contained conflicting messages designed to help them manage conflicting realities. One reality has to do with the shock of being terminated and the impact it can have on one's level of confidence and sense of personal efficacy. One way to cope with the trauma of being terminated is to understand the larger forces at work and how they affect individual circumstances. Of course, there is a danger in explaining away individual situations in terms of macro socio-economic forces. People who rebound and find new positions quickly usually do not see themselves simply as being victims of larger forces. So helping people understand that they are not alone does not extend all the way to suggesting they view themselves solely as victims of uncontrollable circumstances. As a result, the message from the facilitator is one intended to provide comfort (You are not alone! Do not blame yourself.) and, simultaneously, one of self-help (You have the personal means to be captain of your own ship.).

There is another dimension to this situation that sometimes goes unmentioned. As the companies are paying for the service, the facilitator's first allegiance is to the company and not the individual. In most instances this is fine, as the objectives of all parties are essentially the same: to help those in transition find new work as quickly as possible. But what happens when the objectives conflict? What happens when the person in transition wants to sue her former company? People in transition are advised to remember who is paying the bill and keep thoughts about lawsuits to themselves.

But whether the transition services are being paid for by the terminating company or by the individual, transition counselors have a vested interest in sending clients into the job market with a minimum of the anger that so easily accompanies termination. First, people who disparage their former employers are looked upon with skepticism in the marketplace. Most companies are looking for people with positive, can-do attitudes, and shy away from those who appear not to have them. In addition, career counselors advance their own brands by being associated with people who land jobs. Anger management helps that process. But having many people in transition put on a happy face is a serious detriment to taking collective action. Anger is viewed as an essentially dysfunctional emotion, regardless of the circumstances surrounding termination. This is one of many aspects of traditional transition methodologies that need further examination.

The facilitator has spent time with each person explaining the dualism of self-reliance while simultaneously being buffeted about by the external forces of the marketplace. It is a simple concept to grasp and believe in. People like the idea of being liberated from self-blame while being empowered to action through a sense of personal efficacy. Increasingly, however, the tension between the two concepts, and the rather intellectual resolution offered by the facilitator, fails to satisfy all. Those who are into their third and fourth job searches want to know how to avoid being terminated again. They in particular are looking for another good job and are nervous about asking, "Are there any good jobs left?" One might be comforted to know that the answer is: Of course, there are lots of good jobs left, but fewer than there were before. And if the trends hold, there will be even fewer tomorrow. Furthermore, the context that provided us with our current understanding of a good job is itself changing. Tomorrow's good jobs are likely to have much different configurations and employee value propositions. Those jobs are the opportunities that proponents of the new economy talk about as they gaze into the future. How do individuals transition themselves into these new opportunities, and if they cannot, what do they do in the meanwhile? The answers are revealed as individuals in the networking group struggle to land new positions.

A return to the nostalgia of the past would mean for most a return to a time when people could reasonably hope that, once employed, they would retire with the same employer. This would be a time in which retirement parties and engraved watches were scripted routines. But these are different times. Company-financed retirement pay and retiree health care coverage are quickly being replaced with self-financed portable retirement funds and no retiree health care at all. What once appeared to be reliable pension commitments are turning out to be underfunded liabilities that cannot be met.

In addition, responsibility for one's career development has largely shifted from the company to the individual. Workers are now spoken of in terms of human capital, carrying associated costs and productivity. The idea of terminating individual employees for lack of performance has stretched all the way to terminating whole classes of workers whose work is now redundant, too costly, or best done elsewhere or not at all. Understanding how we got here is an important component in understanding the networking meeting about to take place. In some respects the search for a good job is a search for something increasingly rare.

Each member of the group can influence their future and forge their way to the next stage of life. Yet they are all subject to the same economic and social forces of change. This initial meeting of strangers, coming together to discuss their common experiences about losing a job, has itself become a common occurrence.

EMPLOYEE VALUE PROPOSITIONS

The employment value proposition—loyalty to the company in exchange for security of income and career opportunity—has, for large segments of the population, changed forever. The commitment employers are asking from prospective employees often exceeds what companies themselves are willing or able to give. But if we listen to the public relations rhetoric from corporations, it would appear that companies prefer to hire employees who will stay. In turn, employees still prefer to work for companies who take a long-term view of their employment prospects. Some might ask: If both parties want longer-term relationships, why is this not happening? The answer has to do with the competitive pressures in today's marketplace. As it turns out, companies were able to support the rhetoric of mutual loyalty for a relatively short period of time after World War II. Employment for life has morphed into employment for only as long as it is economically feasible for the company. In truth, it probably always has been that way, but just not as obvious.

For example, take a look at how a typical employment offer letter is written today. It is a response to litigation in the 1980s and 1990s, in which terminated employees claimed their terminations were inconsistent with the implied promises companies made during the recruitment process. Language that was once considered appropriate business etiquette such as, "We look forward to your having a great career with us" is now avoided altogether. Successful litigation gave rise to two practices: offer letters with disclaimers of implied contracts; and the inclusion, in some instances, of an agreement to separation benefits as a condition of employment. Negotiated separation benefits happen because the uncertainties of employment tenure are real and very much an ongoing part of the contemporary landscape. As a result, traditional discussions about career and promotional opportunities are not as straightforward as they once were.

Instability of employment, especially at the top, is a hallmark of our time. Depending on which study one reads, the average tenure of CEOs in Canada and the United States is forty months, and moving downward.[1] In terms of job continuity, the level of risk continues to increase. So rather than wait, more senior executives negotiate the terms of their termination before they actually start working.

These are strange times in which we live. Employers and employees alike prefer to hold on to the traditions of past loyalties while being forced to construct employment contracts that pull in the other direction. It is little wonder that those looking for more traditional long-term employment opportunities are confused by what they see and hear. And those who understand the realities of today's job market are in a better position to adjust their expectations and behaviors as they approach the task of finding good jobs.

While some members of the group will try and negotiate the terms of their separation before joining a new company, most will not be able to. The best they will get is an offer letter welcoming them aboard while disclaiming any commitment to a long-term relationship. In conversations with new employees, some corporate recruiters like to dismiss the implied contract language in offer letters as the result of legalese from overzealous lawyers with which they really do not agree and would eliminate it if they could.

The letters have substantial value because they are the first warning signals that the relationship between you and your employer is one of mutual benefit and convenience—for them. When either ceases to exist—convenience or benefit—you are likely to be terminated. Significantly, the threshold for convenience seems much lower than it was a few years ago. The threat of being terminated is real. Terminations have migrated from being acts of last resort to the status of a more value-neutral tool available to employers for containing costs and maintaining competitiveness. In a word, they have become socially acceptable.

There was a time when companies wanted its employees to live in the same community where their work was located. Now it is common for executives to commute thousands of miles to work, returning home on weekends to be with their families. It is common for an employee to accept a position in good faith but quietly keep looking in hopes of finding a better fit. Practices that would have raised eyebrows a few short years ago are finding greater levels of acceptance from employees and employers alike.

The forces giving rise to the evolving relationship between employer and employee are complex and the subject of conflicting interpretations. Some people prefer to explain what is happening in simplistic dichotomous terms. This was the analytical construct Roy and I used when discussing his early retirement. The bad guys came to power and changed the rules. Good guys believe in doing business with a handshake, protecting American jobs, and being loyal to the country. They urge us to keep American jobs at home and buy only those goods made here. But the interplay between these forces is not well informed by good-guy/bad-guy explanations. It is not enough to be dismissive of the morals of people who refuse to take positions on a handshake or accept jobs and keep looking for better ones.

As a nation, and as individual workers, we are in unfamiliar space. Understanding how we got here will allow us negotiate our way through arguably the most turbulent job market we have ever seen. But it is not just an American issue. Participation in a global economy will have implications worldwide. How did we get here, and how do we get from here to the future?

THE AFTERMATH OF WORLD WAR II

To get a better idea of when and how this happened, it is helpful to go back to the post–World War II era. The war and its aftermath is a watershed event in both American and world history. Its effects are with us today. The economy, educational institutions, retirement programs, and the structure of large corporations were all dramatically influenced. By 1940, recovery from the Great Depression of 1929 was well under way. However, unemployment rates were still running at or above 10 percent. Europe was at war, and with the attack on Pearl Harbor, the United States would soon join in. Between 1940 and 1945, America's standing army increased in size from 270,000 to slightly over 8.2 million.[2] As industry transitioned to a wartime economy, the country went from a surplus of labor to a dramatic labor shortage. Almost immediately new workers flooded into the workforce. In the first instance, women were recruited to jobs previously held by men. Traditional stereotypes about jobs and roles appropriate to each gender became blurred under the banner of the war effort. In an earlier time, Rosie the Riveter would have been seen as a woman who did not know her place. Under this rather different circumstance, she emerged as a national hero.

By 1943, women made up 36 percent of the American labor force.[3] Once out of the house and into the factories, there was no going back. And by 1980, according to the Bureau of Labor Statistics, the percentage of women in the civilian non-institutional workforce had grown to a full majority. This movement of women from the home into the workplace was so prevalent that by 1980, a new term, stay-at-home mom, was needed to describe mothers opting not to work outside the home. At this point the reversal was complete. Women were more than just substitutes for men at war. They were a permanent part of the workforce and as such demanded resolution to a long string of workforce equity issues. Can men be given job and pay preferences because they are heads of households? Should women have equal access to education? Can/should women be airline pilots, doctors, CEOs, or U.S. president? All of these seem so obvious now. But at that time they were issues accompanied by strong emotions on both sides.

The other dramatic shift came in the form of minorities and immigrants joining the civilian workforce. World War II touched off a migration of black Americans from the rural South to the industrial centers of the North[4] even greater than that touched off by World War I. As with their white female counterparts, they were intent on becoming a permanent part of the labor pool. Today it is difficult to imagine and easy to forget just how strong a grip racism had on American social life in those times. The idea of African-Americans being full participants in the workforce was unimaginable in the 1940s. There was a story of folkloric proportions about two black soldiers guarding a road gang of German POWs. The white prisoners were allowed to use the whites-only bathroom facilities while their guards were ushered toward the separate and unequal facilities for "coloreds."

The staying power of both minorities and women was aided and abetted by agitation for social change. This resulted in the desegregation of the armed services under Truman, the requirement that government contractors take affirmative action under Kennedy, and the 1964 Civil Rights Act under Johnson. The 1964 Civil Rights Act, among other things, made it illegal to discriminate in employment and promotion practices on the basis of race, sex, religion, or national origin. When the American workforce began contracting, companies were held to the same standards. If not, women and minorities, as the last to be hired, would simply have been the first to be fired. From World War II forward, the ranks of the civilian labor force were permanently swelled by the recruitment and subsequent rising expectations of women and minorities that they rightfully belonged.

The Serviceman's Readjustment Act (GI Bill of Rights) added yet another dimension. GIs returned and received an unprecedented collection of benefits that enhanced their purchasing power, education levels, and career mobility.[5] The drivers behind this were provisions of the act that gave returning servicemen paid education and training, home loan guarantees, and transition compensation of up to fifty-two weeks. GIs could now afford to attend college and compete for jobs in the new economy. They could buy homes many could never have afforded before the war. And they got transition pay to ease their way back into the labor force.

A rapidly expanding economy and advances in technology were the engines of the most impressive job creation boom in American history. The postwar economy was fueled by a pent-up demand for consumer goods. During the war, production of consumer goods was sacrificed to manufacture guns and bombs. But with full employment, there were more and more dollars chasing fewer and fewer goods. During the war, this blueprint for inflation was avoided by controlling prices and wages, and by asking the American public to curtail its demand for certain consumer goods. Rationing commodities such as butter and sponsoring "meatless Tuesdays" were ways of supplying the troops overseas as well as suppressing demand for those goods at home. However, these appeals were unlikely to work in a postwar economy. The answer had to be to begin producing consumer goods for a consumption-hungry population, and conversion to a peacetime, consumer-oriented economy got quickly under way.

At the time of this conversion and for some years to come, there was also a decided lack of competition for markets from other countries. Europe and Japan were preoccupied with reconstructing their nations and economies, and the Soviet Union was undergoing its own internal consolidation under Stalin. In a very real sense, America had the market of the world to itself. These factors came together to absorb the dramatic increase in the supply of labor.

In many respects the post–World War II demand was for workers who had different skill sets than those that existed before the war. As corporations reshaped themselves, they took advantage of organizational structures used so effectively by the military during the war. Ginzberg and Vojta reported:

> On the organizational front, corporations moved to decentralize and divisionalize. At the same time they added planning and control staffs to their expanding headquarters, as well as lower level staffs that were responsible for keeping tabs on the rapidly expanding divisions. In the early years of the post World War II era, the rate of growth of the more successful corporations was often so rapid that the newly expanded staffs had a difficult time just keeping up with and recording the monthly and quarterly gains that were being achieved.[6]

The growth of the postwar labor force created a dramatic increase in white-collar jobs, as noted in earlier chapters. Pent-up demand for consumer goods and access to markets around the world without serious competition from foreign-based companies help create a golden age for the American economy and a competition for workers greater than the numbers of returning GIs, women, and minorities seeking employment.

To compete for their fair share of people, companies began recruiting prospective employees with promises of employment for life, career development, and attractive pensions to finance their retirement years. The cost of these larger staffs and expensive programs could be hidden in the large overhead budgets, or at least deferred for quite some time.[7] The promises to new white-collar recruits of upwardly mobile career opportunities and a lifetime of employment were developed in response to the changing staffing requirements of the corporation and an increased demand for white-collar labor. As the postwar economic boom gathered steam, the value proposition needed to attract this new class of worker was a major factor in the subsequent evolution of benefits.

As competition from abroad increased and economic cycles turned downward, American companies needed higher levels of productivity to remain competitive. In addition, advances in technology were making it possible for companies to be managed with fewer workers and flatter organizations.

One of the first practices to come under scrutiny was the traditional way companies handled redundant white-collar workers. When they were fewer in number, the normal practice was to hide them in staff jobs doing unessential work. It was one thing to hide the occasional misfit, as my father-in-law had, but quite another to hide an entire class of workers. As the demand for increased efficiencies grew along with the numbers of white-collar workers, traditional remedies became unacceptably expensive.

The birth of the career transition/outplacement business can be traced to the growing need of companies to trim their workforces and improve productivity. The first corporate purchase of job search services is reputed to have come from Humble Oil in New Jersey in the 1960s, when the automation of a local refinery created several redundant positions among supervisors and lab technicians. After a full year with no success in finding suitable positions, those who were still without jobs were slated for termination.[8] By today's standards, keeping workers without jobs on the payroll for a full year and then providing them with severance and outplacement support seems generous. But then, such separations were not the norm and required careful handling. Humble hired job search counselors to see if their services could be used to provide job placement support. Much to everyone's relief and perhaps surprise, all terminated employees were placed within ninety days.

In 1969, Thomas Hubbard, Inc. (THINC) was founded to deal primarily with outplaced executives. Quickly, however, pressure grew to provide outplacement support to the entire population of displaced white-collar workers. In an attempt to manage their legal exposures, and in response to the favorable tax treatment of expenses associated with workforce restructuring, corporations started to extend outplacement benefits to broader segments of the employee population and did adverse-impact analyses to make sure certain protected groups were not being disproportionately affected by layoffs.

The first such broad application of outplacement support came in 1978 from an insurance firm headquartered on the East Coast.[9] In seemingly no time at all, the use of outplacement as a management tool caught on throughout the country, and later the entire industrialized world. The changing landscape of corporations gave rise to a new industry and a new set of experiences for their workers. Companies such as IBM held on to the old order as long as they could and vowed never to have a general layoff.

A GLOBALIZED WORLD

Just as the outplacement industry was maturing in the 1990s, the global economy gathered steam. American jobs were on the move, which created an active debate about the implications of a more global economy. Some argued that the outsourcing and offshoring of work was destroying American jobs as well as those in Japan, Germany, England, and France. A variety of sources, including the McKinsey Global Institute, predicted a precipitous rise of from 30 to 40 percent a year in the numbers of jobs being sent to other countries. However, once one gets inside the numbers, argues Daniel Denzer, they find that:

> Even if the most dire-sounding forecasts come true, the impact on the economy will be negligible. [One] prediction of 3.3 million lost jobs for example, is spread across 15 years. That would mean 220,000 jobs displaced per year by offshore outsourcing—a number that sounds impressive until one considers that total employment in the United States is roughly 130 million and that about 22 million new jobs are expected to be added between now and 2010. Annually, outsourcing would affect less than 2 percent of employed Americans.[10]

Denzer and others note that the fall in manufacturing jobs has more to do with technology than with offshoring. More work being done by fewer people affects not just American jobs, but jobs anywhere in the world.

Regardless of what side of the debate one comes down on, the economic and technological revolution before us will have significant consequences. And the debate is not so much about how goods and services will be produced, but where and by whom. It is now clear that an extraordinary portion of the American GNP is weightless. As John Heilmann observed:

> The information economy has arrived. More Americans make computers than cars; more make semiconductors than construction machinery; more work in communications gear than all other capital equipment combined. Software is the country's fastest growing industry. World trade in information-related goods and services is growing five times faster than in natural resources.[11]

Frances Cairncross made the observation that we are in the midst of the *Death of Distance* in which the lack of limitation on "virtually free electronic communications and the fall of barriers to trade and investment flows will transform patterns of economic activity."[12]

Questions about where goods will be produced and by whom have been spurred by geopolitical forces. The breakup of the former Soviet Union, the coming of age of India, and the entrance of China into the global marketplace means that since the 1980s there has been an increasing need for the integration of nearly 2.5 billion people into the world economy, "many millions of whom are highly skilled."[13] It is clear that globalization and technology have combined to make goods and services cheaper and ubiquitously available. A refusal to let jobs migrate to where they can be performed most efficiently is a difficult position to maintain. It would require selling goods and services on the global market with a higher cost of production than similar goods produced in more economically rational places. Consumers are not likely to cooperate by paying higher prices just because goods have been made in America. If offshoring and outsourcing become industry best practices, companies that do not participate run the risk of being marginalized out of existence. Companies are creating more efficient and cost-effective organizational structures along with politics aimed at retaining only the most desirable employees. Work is being shifted to wherever it makes sense to have it performed. There was a time when American leaders thought what was good for General Motors was good for America—a time in which the interests of the white-collar worker and that of the company were the same. As it turns out, those interests were coincidental, not identical.

Areas of agreement about globalization include the reality that the nature of work throughout the world is changing rapidly and right before our eyes. While traditional jobs still exist, there are fewer of them, and the new jobs being created look very different than the jobs that went before.

The work many of us are presently doing can be done elsewhere at less cost, with greater efficiency, and by someone who is happy to take lower pay and fewer benefits. Furthermore, companies that fail to take advantage of more cost-effective industry best practices risk losing their ability to compete.

Corporations are today what they have always been—self-interested economic entities seeking to maximize profits for their owners. What changed are the ways it gets that done. During World War II, American corporations were willing instruments of national policy. After the war they were again more the instruments of their shareholders. Technology allowed work to be re-engineered, and fewer people were needed to produce the same amount. At an earlier time companies would have been reluctant to let people go. But when the numbers of excess people became much too large, corporate mores shifted to accommodate their evolving reality. Two additional changes hastened the movement toward a more disposable worker: Advances in technology made doing work anywhere in the world possible, and globalization made it absolutely necessary.

That is how we got here, and here is the present-day reality: Large numbers of people are between jobs, have been between jobs, or know of someone who is. Those entering the workforce for the first time are facing a world quite different from the one their grandparents faced. Instead of the unbridled optimism of an expanding postwar economy, their offers of employment will likely contain carefully scripted stipulations about not intending to make implied promises.

That is the reality facing this networking group as they meet and try to put their lives back together. Their job searches are being led by an industry that has allowed itself to be defined by the net sum of its tools—résumé writing, networking, and the development of traditional interviewing skills. We now have a generation of workers that has been between jobs more than once. Corporations are beginning to view the job transition process as a commodity requiring little more than a refresher course to get terminated employees ready for transition. They are buying the services of outplacement firms for shorter periods of time for each employee and at less unit cost. Meanwhile, those in transition are being encouraged to go quietly into the night during a time of revolutionary change.

The group has much in common in the midst of mixed emotions. Some are sad, others are angry. Some are nervous while still others have been here before. They do not know whether to blame themselves or their companies for this uncomfortable circumstance. But one thing is certain: How they handle this situation and what they understand about it will impact their ability to find meaningful work. Handling it correctly means uncovering new tools and preparing themselves for a job market with which they may not be familiar. Otherwise they will likely become mired in a seeming endless regression of jobs that do not last and with employers who do not seem to care. The insight they gain about themselves and others can begin to prepare them for a brave new world of work. But failure to learn will result in being stuck in a time warp in which they search for jobs from a by-gone era without fully understanding how portable their jobs have become or that they are now members of an increasingly disposable workforce.

AND THE GROUP IS LED BY...

Mary Parsons is the group's facilitator and a ten-year employee of the out-placement firm hired to assist these seven strangers with their transitions. She is about to join the group, which has already gathered in the conference room. As is sometimes the case, Mary spent part of her morning contemplating her own personal journey into the outplacement profession. She fell into this line of work without giving a single thought to its history or to the reality that it is a relatively new profession. She started her career in human resources and took time off to raise two children. Her new profession is rewarding, well beyond her initial expectations, because she acts as a catalyst for the personal growth of her clients. The very nature of the job search process is an opportunity for people to know themselves better and regain confidence. They learn how easily their confidence can be fractured, and the process by which it can be regained. Mary interacts with people at a time when they need her help the most. She derives personal satisfaction as she helps people come to grips with their current situation and move on to the next stage as quickly as possible. Even after ten years at the job, she is surprised at how quickly some move on and how others linger jobless much too long.

Many of the people she worked with are truly grateful for her services and often stay in touch long after the group ceases to function. In this respect Mary and her clients share a mutual understanding of the importance of work and the role it plays in all their lives. Having gone through her own job transition, Mary knows that the match between her personal needs and the rewards of being a career counselor, for her, is just about as good as it gets.

What she looked for earlier in her career is in stark contrast to what she does today. Some of the change in perspective is a reflection of her personal maturation. Much of it also is a function of the changing landscape of the world of work.

Mary's first position out of college was with a large multinational company. Her first twenty-four months were to be spent on a series of rotational as-signments designed to give her an overview of the different functions within the organization and an opportunity to make a personal choice about what might be the best fit for her. During this time she relocated to three different states. These moves were not burdensomely expensive for the company. There was almost no movement of household goods or any closing costs on real estate. In addition to the sheer fun and excitement of it, these rotating as-signments also met several company objectives as well. Employees would be given a thorough orientation and have a better understanding of the company and its culture. It would also provide management with performance data, and those who did not fit could be encouraged to move on to opportunities elsewhere. Still, Mary thought to herself more than once that carrying employees on payroll for two full years without them making a direct contribution seemed like a waste of resources. But that was not for her to decide.

The company also used trainees to do college recruiting. Students were likely impressed by the experiences and opportunities being fed back to them by recent graduates. The leave-behind recruitment literature referred to future recruits as an "entering class" and "company leaders of tomorrow." It was an implied set of promises that now have a familiar and fading ring. "Come with us," they told her, "you'll have a great future working here."

About a year and a half into the program, Mary's company fell on hard times. Intensifying foreign competition, changing consumer preferences, and a world recession forced them to rethink programs like the one Mary was recruited to. As the economic environment worsened and the company's earnings per share and stock price declined, the program was terminated. Offers extended to the next class were rescinded. In their stead the company announced a mandated 15 percent across-the-board budget and head count reduction. Even though Mary's training rotations were not complete, her position was eliminated as she got her first real taste of the new corporate ethic. A few members of Mary's class were retained; mostly those who had been placed in permanent jobs before their twenty-four-month trainee period was up. They were either considered the best and brightest of that class or were viewed as having friends in high places.

The experience shook Mary's confidence, and she began wondering what she could have done to effect a different outcome. She also became aware of being caught up in a sea of change affecting the way corporations looked after their economic self-interests. Rather than see herself as a victim, Mary chose to focus on the choices in front of her and how those choices impacted the environment in which she found herself. She moved on.

BOB WATSON'S TERMINATION

Bob Watson is a member of the networking group whose position elimination was both ironic and typical. In his capacity as director of operations control for an engineering firm, he had been asked to join a special projects team to look into the rising level of customer attrition. The firm, Design Engineering (not its real name), had been in existence for over fifty years and relied heavily on repeat business. The original founders believed that a satisfied and well-informed customer was the backbone of new business development. Over the years, Design became known for the quality of its work and the great length its people went to in order to satisfy customers. Any firm hoping to compete in its space needed to establish and maintain the same standards. For many years this kind of market leadership meant that all of Design's competitors had similar cost structures and profit margins.

During the last decade, new trends emerged. First, loyal customers that had routinely given Design their business were more and more insisting on a formal bidding process. This was initially attributed to the Sarbanes-Oxley bill passed by Congress in the wake of the Enron scandal, requiring corporations to document their internal control processes. This gave accountants and purchasing professionals greater say in how companies purchased goods and services. No one at Design was particularly concerned because they believed that the quality of their work deserved a premium in price.

Design's senior management was caught by surprise when they began losing more than half of their bid projects. At first they suspected that competitors were buying market share by pricing certain projects at cost. To them, it was a mini-version of the cola wars. They decided to play the game by submitting bids down to the level of the competition, with little or no profit margin. Two things happened: They did not make much money on the bids they won, and they kept losing bids.

The project team decided to do a postmortem of lost bids by interviewing purchasing managers. While none were willing to provide detailed bid information, most were willing to acknowledge that Design's bids were substantially off the mark. Bob's fellow team members first thought the competition was not only taking the profit out of its bids, but actually willing to do the work at a loss. That made no sense, and they knew it.

Bob was among the first inside Design to figure out what had happened. The long-standing practice of relying on repeat business and word-of-mouth had left the company without any significant business development acumen. They did not know how to drum up new business because they had never had to. As a result, the firm had become somewhat insulated from important market trends.

A couple of competitors in particular had been able to outsource and offshore much of the work done by Bob's department as well as several others. This created a twin benefit difficult to overcome. Competitors were able to reduce their costs of production by a minimum of 20 percent. Because their work was shipped electronically around the world, they were also able to provide a forty-eight-hour turnaround time, a huge advantage over the accepted industry standard of five business days. This combination of lower prices and improved customer service could not be overcome by Design's traditional customer loyalties.

Once the project team reported its findings, Bob knew that major organizational and structural changes were on the way. He sensed correctly that his job and those of many of his colleagues were at risk. At first he thought they would figure out a way to keep him. After all, he had been with the firm a long time and had risen handsomely through the ranks. But in the end he knew better and began preparing himself emotionally for what was to come. Still, on the day he was told, his termination came as a shock. He was more disappointed than angry—disappointed that those whom he knew so well were not able or willing to give him the speech he wanted to hear. "Bob, we're laying off a lot of people, but the value you bring to this firm is so obvious, we will figure out a way to keep you on." I suppose that happens to some people. But for so many others that speech is never given, and termination feels a lot more personal than it really is.

Bob's one-on-one with Mary was designed to be like the others she'd had with individuals in the group as well as with the hundreds of others she had seen over the years. She would first assess how ready Bob was to move on, provide him with an overview of the transition process, and let him know about the networking group. Over the past year or so Mary had sensed that her clients were in a different place compared to an earlier time. For one thing, fewer were angry at their employer. This probably had to do with companies getting better at the termination process. But it also resulted from terminations being so much more the accepted norm. Though still painful, they were more common.

The original tools developed within the career transition industry were designed in part to help people manage the personal trauma of termination. Though some people continue to need help with anger control and skills like résumé writing, they soon may demand more. Bob Watson was a case in point.

He interrupted Mary's inquiry to explain that he had seen this coming, but was unable to do anything about it. Now that he is looking for another job, he needed help understanding what had just happened to him and what his value is in the marketplace today. He knows what he does for a living can now be done by others at a different price point. He also suspects there are other jobs out there just like the one he left. But he wants help positioning himself in the marketplace in a way that is less subject to what he just went through. He asked Mary whether her tools and methodologies will help him do that.

That conversation took place a couple of days prior to today's networking meeting and confirmed Mary's suspicion that the now thirty-year-old career transition methodologies she had been using were about to atrophy. New concepts were required. This raised several new questions, most of which she did not have the answers to. If she could enlist this group in a discussion of the issues, perhaps together they could begin to develop them. Mary began to realize that her career had been subject to the same set of issues. The difference is, globalization has gathered momentum and its effects are more readily recognizable.

She had already asked the other group members to be prepared to use the elevator-speech format to introduce themselves. Traditionally, this speech serves two purposes. It helps people present their situations to others comfortably and facilitates clarity about what they want from others as they engage them in their cause. Any speech that takes longer than the typical elevator ride is considered too long and will likely lose the attention of the listener. Mary has asked Bob to be prepared to go first and act as a catalyst to help this group face a job market increasingly dominated by the new economy.

The room grows quiet as Mary begins her introductory remarks.

"Good morning. As a reminder, I am Mary Parsons, and I have invited all of you individually to meet today in an effort to move forward with the job search process. In a moment I will ask each of you, beginning with Bob Watson, to introduce yourselves using the sixty-second elevator-speech format. Before that, however, I thought it would be helpful to review the process we will use until landing another position and what to do after that."

Mary was aware of the different levels of anxiety and skepticism in the group. She spoke of finding a new position matter-of-factly to encourage confidence that it can be done. She also knew the words "what to do after that" would pique their collective curiosity and lay the foundation for transforming their individual job searches into a lifelong career management process. Beyond that, she felt like a broken record. She had given this speech many times, always believing the job search process conformed to the same indisputable rules: A good story about why you are out of work, a well-written résumé, and good networking contacts equaled reemployment in the near future. Clients were then counseled to keep networking even after having found a job. However, almost none of her clients followed the post-landing networking advice, and they are now finding it more difficult than ever to find good jobs. Maybe it is time to do something different.

"Good morning. My name is Bob Watson and about a year ago a funny thing happened to me on the way to work. I figured out my job was going to be outsourced to India and there was nothing I could do about it. Until just recently I was the director of design operations, where I managed a team responsible for tracking design development and implementation. The division of labor we used for the past several years has not kept up with the market. If the company is to survive, it must take advantage of industry best practices, and that means finding more efficient ways of operating.

"Once I got over the shock of understanding that it was my job that was being eliminated, I wondered what kind of job I would look for next. Should I go to work for a company that doesn't believe in outsourcing? How about a company that promises to never lay people off?

"When I told my son my job was being outsourced, he asked if he should stop studying engineering at the university. I told him that did not seem like a good idea just now. I said, as you start your career and I continue mine, we should for now just try and figure out what questions to ask. It is hard to get to the right answers unless you at least have the right questions. And right now I am about to join a networking group of people who are in the same boat I am. Maybe together we can figure out what is happening to our economy and whether there are any good jobs left."

CHAPTER FOUR

✾

ARE THERE ANY GOOD JOBS LEFT?

THE QUESTION BOB Watson asked is simple enough. The answer is more complex. Questions about the availability of good jobs have profound implications because they raise doubts about the continuing availability of the American dream—a dream that has been a powerful source of inspiration and social stability. It was a dream expanded after World War II to include women and minorities. The mere suggestion that it may no longer be attainable is cause for concern.

I recently invited myself into a conversation three men were having about being unemployed and their difficulty finding suitable work. One was particularly animated. His training in accounting had allowed him to land a couple of teaching assignments (adjunct professorships), but he had been unable to come anywhere near his previous income.

I took note of how much of his life—and the lives of others I have spoken with—was structured around the expectation of having a good job. He had completely bought into most of what that had come to mean. He had kids in college, a second mortgage, and monthly debt obligations that easily consumed his cash flow. Now, with no prospects of a job in sight, health care premiums he could not afford, and more debt than he could carry, the world he had grown to trust had disappeared. His version of the American dream had turned into an American nightmare. As we talked, it became clear that he did not want just another job. He wanted his dignity back. He wanted his old sense of having a job and a career that others respected. He wanted another good job.

One feature of a good job relates to the continuity of work and its associated income. It allows us to do things such as take on long-term debt. How much debt as well as the length of the debt obligations is often a function of monthly cash flow. Interruptions to a person's income can easily interrupt access to the American dream. And the potential for such interruptions grew for Americans as terminations migrated from being tools of last resort to socially acceptable ways of controlling costs.

European countries have been more aggressive in providing safety nets for their workers. The machinery for laying workers off is more complex and difficult for employers to navigate. Once completed, companies are required to pay extended severance depending on how long the employee had worked there. The United Auto Workers (UAW) negotiated a similar salary continuation package for its members displaced by plant closings. Automobile manufacturers are required to carry full salary and benefit costs for workers up to three years. How sustainable this arrangement will be is unclear. It is reasonable to expect that these jobs will be candidates for being sent offshore to more economically rational locations. This is one of several factors influencing the current turmoil in the auto industry. Most white-collar workers have little if any protection at all.

The companies for whom we work provide access to the American system of health care and to company-financed pensions. For millions of white-collar workers, this has meant that treatment for serious illness has been available without inviting personal economic ruin. People could get sick, survive, and even retire in relative economic comfort.

For several generations of white-collar workers, this is all they have ever known. While it is difficult to imagine how people got along without these things, none of them existed to any significant degree before World War II. For unionized workers these benefits were the result of hard-won victories and bitter battles long faded from the conscience of today's public. For the burgeoning white-collar masses, they were largely extended to them as protection against further unionization and as key elements in the post–World War II war for talent. This package of promises is the employment value proposition that companies offered in exchange for the loyalty of its workers. This was an exchange in which a company's reputation (employment brand) became critically important.

IBM, General Electric, General Motors, Ford, PepsiCo, and many other companies have carefully guarded their product and employment brands. What these companies became known for were the reasons people purchased their products and applied for their jobs. Good companies were the ones with the good jobs, and having one of those jobs, especially following the Great Depression, was a source of personal pride.

The transition to a white-collar workforce also became a transition to a reliance on companies to provide the context in which we live and an important source of our sense of economic well-being. The well-being and self-interest of individual workers were seen as being synonymous with that of the corporation. It was in this context that Charles Wilson, president of General Motors from 1941 to 1953, proudly claimed, "What is good for General Motors is good for the United States."

Having a good job was more than an ego boost. The very patterns of our lives were shaped by the jobs at which we worked. If the Social Security system reduced the threat of poverty in old age, company-funded pensions and retiree health care coverage made it possible to retire with virtually no diminution of living standard at all. The expectation was that our jobs would last a lifetime, but if not, other good jobs were near at hand. In addition, there was always the hope we could continue to move up the organization ladder through company-sponsored career development programs. This gave workers a comfortable mind-set to use in structuring their lives.

These programs seemed logical and affordable when first started. It appeared to be a perfect coincidence of interest between our jobs and us. GM highlighted how unaffordable these programs have become when its management announced in 2005 that it was spending more on health care than on the steel in each General Motors' car.[1] These realities were part of GM's insistence on becoming more global and establishing the capability to manufacture automobiles anywhere in the world. Its operating cost structure was one it could not afford indefinitely.

Carly Fiorina, former CEO of Hewlett-Packard, sent chills through the collective American mind when she commented, "No American has a God-given right to a job." While this may not have come as surprise to the rest of the world, it is not the way Americans had learned to think. And it seemed to confirm what others were beginning to believe: Good jobs, especially those in America were disappearing.

Access to good jobs is a key motivator behind educating ourselves and our children. We structure our debts and dreams through our jobs. And there is a presumption of the availability of the American dream that has dominated the American mind for a long time. World War II gave a particular shape to how the dream would be accessed. Globalization is now the primary force behind how we will need to access it for generations to come. The reshaping of American jobs is different from what happened following the war.

Lou Dobbs, anchor and managing editor of CNN's *Lou Dobbs Tonight,* has been a forceful advocate for the position that corporate greed is the major force behind the disappearance of jobs from America, which he labels an assault on the middle class. In his book *Exporting America,* he cites numerous examples of jobs being exported elsewhere because of, among other things, cheaper labor costs. He cites these examples:

- Carrier moving over 1,200 jobs to Asia, and of New York State losing over 10,000 jobs since 1990.
- Tower Automotive in Milwaukee moving 500 jobs to Mexico as indicative of the 200,000 fewer jobs in the automotive industry in the past four years.
- Maytag moving jobs to Mexico, citing competition from cheaper appliances made elsewhere.
- Travelocity shutting down 250 jobs in a town of 1,800 and moving them to India.
- The Smithsonian outsourcing the development of its online library system to a firm that outsourced the work to the Philippines.[2]

At one time the emergence of the biotechnology industry was seen as the savior to jobs being lost in California's Silicon Valley. Now "there are signs that the nation's biotech industry may be on the verge of an offshoring wave of its own."[3] The reasons? The cost of doing business elsewhere is pennies on the dollar without sacrificing access to some of the best minds in the industry.

Though several American presidents actively supported the North American Free Trade Agreement (NAFTA), other political leaders have blamed it for the jobless recovery from the last recession. Ross Perot during his run as an independent candidate for president in 1992 advised that if NAFTA were passed, the "great sucking sound we would hear is the rush of American jobs going to Mexico." The movement of jobs to more cost-efficient locations is seen as part and parcel of a trend from the 1970s in which back-office service operations were moved out of costly urban centers (New York City, for example) to less costly rural areas such as South Dakota and the American South. Moving these jobs still further to Asia, Mexico, and elsewhere is seen as a continuation of this same trend. Furthermore, it is a trend that affects not only the United States, but any nation and industry in which there are more cost-effective alternatives.

The proponents of offshoring have come to the following conclusions:

- Job losses in manufacturing are a function of technology.
- Offshoring accounts for a small percentage of jobs in America.
- Moving jobs to cheaper, more efficient venues is the continuation of long-established trends.

The Bureau of Labor Statistics began tracking jobs lost due to the relocation of work and reported only slightly more than 4,600 in the first quarter of 2004, which was just 2.5 percent of total layoffs in the quarter.[4] By this measure, offshoring would not appear as a serious threat to jobs.

Comparisons to European countries yield similar conclusions and evidence that Americans may actually have the right idea. Jacob Kirkegaard, of the Institute for International Economics, made the observation that offshoring in Europe will actually end in the creation of greater wealth and more jobs for Europeans, which means a net gain in employment. He acknowledges that workers whose jobs are sent offshore are the losers in this transaction, but countries losing jobs this way as a whole gain. The obstacle to a globally competitive Europe—an obstacle the United States does not have—"is by far the inflexibility of many of Europe's labor markets, where many layers of employment protection legislation and likely court interferences prevent layoffs and thus ultimately new hiring of workers."[5]

The magnitude of the issues facing American-based automotive manufacturers was revealed in 2005 when Delphi, the largest auto supply company in the world and a spin-off from GM, declared bankruptcy. Delphi's labor contracts (which closely mirror those of GM) called for their highest union wages to pay out at $65 per hour ($28 in direct wages and $37 in benefits).

Both GM and Delphi announced multiple plant closings and major union givebacks as necessary conditions to restoring their economic health. Each of the big three automakers has also announced major reductions in their white-collar workforce, with Ford leading the way with promised reductions of as much as 30 percent. Their problems are shaped by a high cost of labor that is not globally competitive, which affects the entire spectrum of jobs, union and nonunion alike.

In contrast, Continental (a German-based auto parts supplier) reported an earnings jump of 36 percent and a 60 percent rise in its stock price in the first nine months of 2005. At first glance it would appear that the success of a German-based company vis-à-vis Delphi flies in the face of earlier discussions about redeployable workforces. According to Manfred Wennemer, Continental's CEO, their formula for success actually reinforces the point. Continental is profitable because:

- 61 percent of its 81,000 employers work outside of Germany, mostly in countries like Brazil, Romania, and China, where labor is more reasonably priced and redeployable.
- Fewer than 15 percent work in the United States.
- They make no apologies to German workers for moving jobs elsewhere because redeployment is good for everyone in the long run.[6]

In other words, their success has come from using globalization to their advantage and letting go many of the traditional constraints imposed by nationalism.

Under the global scenario for success, it is helpful to understand what happens to jobs. First, they migrate to more economically rational places. Other jobs, that at one time would have been created as a part of the economic multiplier effect, never get created in their "home" countries. This migration of jobs and opportunities forces those who would have otherwise occupied them to be redeployed to other opportunities that, in turn, have been shaped by the marketplace. These are jobs that may not have any of the elements of the good jobs Americans went to college to get.

When companies compete globally they are obliged to match the efficiencies and best practices of other global competitors producing similar goods and services. To the extent that offshore outsourcing becomes an accepted means of moving jobs to more economically rational locations, it also becomes a best practice. Companies that do not follow suit risk losing their ability to compete. This dynamic is a major force among automobile manufacturers today and has already spread to other sectors of the global economy. But when jobs go elsewhere their movement creates an inevitable pool of workers in need of redeployment.

However, the very things American white-collar workers are concerned about—being outsourced, downsized, and let go—are viewed by some as competitive advantages. A flexible workforce is one that can be redeployed to other high-end jobs created as a result of the global economy. This assumption rests on a general belief that the only jobs being sent offshore are those at the lower end of the technology spectrum. The good jobs—those involving technology innovation—would stay. According to an article in the March 21, 2005, issue of *Business Week,* "that pledge is now passé." Companies like Motorola, Dell, Philips, and others are buying complete designs in an attempt to lower their R&D costs, and a new structure of the modern corporation is beginning to emerge.[7] Companies are beginning to establish a global network of partners, no one of which may have America's national interests or the interests of the American worker at the center of its concerns. That is, the modern corporation is unlikely to be an effective conduit for national interests.

For now, the numbers of jobs going offshore are more than offset by the numbers of jobs being created as companies put their capital to different and more profitable uses. The jobs that go away come back in the form of jobs requiring higher levels of skills, and with the creation of greater value than those that left.

However, there does appear to be an ongoing understatement of what happens to the individuals in these instances. It is as if the creation of more jobs at higher levels automatically assuages those who are negatively impacted. Their skills are neither automatically upgraded, nor are their transitions to new employment buffered in recognition of their displacement. Furthermore, the European model of making layoffs difficult may be among the worst choices available to the United States because it decreases the ability of companies/countries to redeploy workers and thereby participate more fully in the global economy. That being said, the current number of jobs going offshore is but a fraction of the American GNP and will likely stay that way for a while longer.

As it currently stands, the threat to American jobs, though perhaps more real than some are willing to acknowledge, does not appear to be the immediate catastrophe suggested in the popular press. The matter does not end there, and the answer to the availability of jobs is less obvious than an arithmetic calculation implies. To understand why, it is helpful to explore the differences in context between being employed in America today as compared with thirty years ago. These differences define how jobs are being created as well as what having a good job means. Humble Oil made sure its excess personnel were transitioned successfully to other good jobs. A few years later, my father-in-law Roy was forced into early retirement. There was no real threat to his standard of living or to any of the retiree health benefits he had been promised. In a sense, he was simply being paid not to work.

One gets the impression that neither Humble Oil nor Roy's company was particularly proud of having to take these actions. The idea of moving to more cost-effective modes of operation by laying off entire classes of white-collar workers had not yet become an accepted business practice. Moving operations from one state to another in the name of efficiency was still looked on as a violation of community and individual trust.

But by the time Jack Welch was in charge at GE, he could eliminate 81,000 jobs and become a self-proclaimed hero. How is it that terminating the employment of otherwise productive workers is now the stuff of which heroes is made when earlier it was considered a violation of trust? Did our morals change?

In a sense our morals did change, but only after there was a change in context—a context that created a mind-set and collective thought pattern for an entire nation. Understanding that phenomenon is a key to understanding the mind-set shift that individuals will need as they begin competing in the new economy.

The way American-based companies are implementing globalization is at odds with what they were entrusted with following World War II. This explains why globalization feels different from what has gone before and why corrective public policy will likely lag seriously behind the problems globalization creates for American workers. Furthermore, the inability to recognize what is different about globalization will lead people to conduct job searches and do career planning in ways that miss their marks.

Advocates and critics of globalization appear to be looking at it with different lenses, which may explain how they come to such different conclusions. Malcolm Gladwell referred to the different perspectives on similar phenomena as the "Power of Context."[8] By this he means that events are "sensitive to the conditions and circumstances of the times and places in which they occur." For example, the New York City crime wave of the 1980s became exaggerated because of "little things" in the environment that seemingly gave people permission to commit criminal behavior, and not because there were more criminals. It was the context in which crime was taking place that explained the increased levels of criminal behavior. It was the same contextual power that explained the behavior of seminary students as they dealt with a study reenacting the Parable of the Good Samaritan:

> [The researchers] met with a group of seminarians individually, and asked each one to prepare a short, extemporaneous talk on a given biblical theme, then walk over to a nearby building and present it. Along the way to the presentation, each student ran into a man slumped in an alley, head down, eyes closed, coughing and groaning. The question was: Who would stop and help?[9]

The most powerful predictor of who would stop had less to do with the individual morals of individual students and more to do with what was said to them before they left for the other building. "In some of the cases . . . the experimenter would look at his watch and say, 'Oh, you're late. They were expecting you a few minutes ago. We'd better get moving.' In other cases, he would say, 'It will be a few minutes before they're ready for you, but you might as well head over now.' This latter group was significantly more likely to stop. Indeed, on several occasions, a seminary student going to give his talk on the Parable of the Good Samaritan literally stepped over the victim as he hurried on his way."

In New York City, the police and Transit Authority changed the context in which crime was happening. They cleaned up the graffiti-smeared trains, arrested turnstile jumpers, and generally became less tolerant of "quality of life" crimes. "After a while, the bad guys wised up and began to leave their weapons home and paid their fares." Crime in NYC dropped precipitously.[10]

It is interesting that the behaviors of criminals and seminary students are better explained by the context in which they take place than by self-professed morals. It is context that gives permission to act one way versus another. And permission eventually becomes its own justification. The same is true of organizations.

Let us revisit Humble Oil's decision on how to handle its excess employees. Why did Humble work so hard to find jobs for its people? In part it was because more was at stake than a few people losing and then finding work. These were members of a white-collar workforce who had been recruited with certain expectations in mind that were part of a larger context of a socially acceptable employment value proposition. To keep Humble from being in violation of its trust, it was important for all affected employees to transition seamlessly to other employment.

By the time Welch was imposing his will on GE, shedding excess workers had become a more acceptable way of doing business. After all, terminating the employment of otherwise productive people did not mean they were being relegated forever to a status of unemployment. They could find new jobs of comparable worth. However, the context for employment had changed.

What is happening to employment in America is only partially revealed by the numbers of jobs that disappear. The statistics do not comfortably support any of the extremes we have discussed. It is not simply a matter of greedy corporations moving jobs elsewhere. And while the percentage of jobs affected is comparatively small, the shift in context is significant and deserves attention. The context in which acceptable employment value propositions are forged for white-collar workers has changed. That has changed the patterns of our jobs and the mind-set we need to manage our lives.

It is context that gives permission. And as new socially acceptable employment value propositions evolve, the question arises: What has this new context given companies permission to do? To find out, it is helpful to take a closer look at how the elements of our jobs continue to change and why the jobs that replace them may not be of comparable worth.

SOME ECONOMICS OF HEALTH CARE

The health care insurance system in the United States is unique among industrialized nations. It is a system that rations care on the basis of the ability to pay rather than on clinical need. It is among the most expensive systems in the world for individuals to access because of duplication of services offered, the performance of unnecessary procedures, and the ineffective use of some technologies.[11] Among the top twenty-four industrialized nations, the United States ranks twenty-first in infant mortality and sixteenth in life expectancy. People without jobs or working for companies that do not offer health care coverage usually cannot afford private insurance. Over 43 million Americans have no coverage at all.[12] Yet, President George W. Bush calls it the best system in the world.

As a result of globalization, corporations looking to compete on a global stage are joining the ranks of those who also cannot afford the American health care system. Access to health care has not always been too expensive, and there was a time when private insurance companies had no interest in getting into the health care insurance business because no one was spending money either on getting well or on trying to avoid getting sick. This was largely before hospitals took their current form as places to go for treatment. Until then, children were born at home and surgery was avoided altogether. But if surgery was unavoidable, it also was done at home.

A "1918 Bureau of Labor Statistics (BLS) survey of 211 families living in Columbus Ohio found that only 7.6 [percent] of their average annual medical expenses paid for hospital care."[13] The most significant financial threat came from lost wages due to illness rather than the cost of health care.

Several factors combined to raise the cost of care while simultaneously extending health care coverage to a large portion of the American public. First, medical care simply got better because of higher licensing standards for physicians, improvements in medical technology, and the ability of hospitals to provide sterilized environments. These factors coalesced to drive the demand for medical care to all-time highs throughout the industrialized world.

Higher standards also were responsible for the dramatic decrease of 38 percent in the number of medical schools in the United States between 1910 and 1922. Schools that could not/did not meet the newly imposed standards were closed, as they could not longer graduate physicians approved for practice. Hospital costs began to rise, and by 1934 was reported to be 40 percent of a family's medical expenses when hospitalization was involved.

Major leaps in medical technology made access to medical care more important than ever before, and people in the industrialized nations of the world began agitating for systematic access to health care insurance. Most countries opted for nationalized systems in which health care is based on clinical need. But in the United States, a system developed based on the ability to pay.

Four primary factors account for the development of the health care system of coverage in America: the founding of Blue Cross/Blue Shield practices; the growth of private insurers; government policy; and the American Medical Association (AMA).

The Blue Cross/Blue Shield practices were innovations in the methods of payment, in that medical expenses (Blue Cross for hospitals and Blue Shield for physician services) for the first time were prepaid on a per capita group plan basis. That is, all members of a group of employees were insured on a per capita basis, and if a member was hospitalized or in need of physician services, the fees were paid. The genesis of modern health care insurance is generally considered to have been created by J. F. Kimball, who in 1929:

> As a former school superintendent [he] became an administrator at Baylor Hospital in Dallas [and] . . . found himself confronting some of the same problems he'd faced as an educator. Reviewing the unpaid accounts receivable of Baylor hospital, [he] recognized many names of Dallas school teachers.
>
> Knowing well from experience that these low paid teachers would never be able to pay their bills, he initiated the not-for-profit Baylor Plan which allowed teachers to pay 50 cents a month into a fund that guaranteed up to 21 days of hospital care at Baylor Hospital. The Baylor Plan—the genesis of modern health insurance— sparked interest in hospitals across the country, as they scrambled to set up similar plans. In 1944, the Baylor Plan was merged into the Texas institution we know today as Blue Cross and Blue Shield of Texas.[14]

From the very beginning, this system benefited individual group members (because of the affordable rates) and hospitals and physicians (because of essentially guaranteed/collectable income streams). Private insurers had initially avoided the health care business because they thought policies pursued on an individual basis would have the problem of adverse selection. That is, only sick people would want policies. That same reasoning is why individual policies remain out of reach for people out of work today. In contrast, the Baylor Plan (and later the entire BC/BS system) extended coverage to relatively young and healthy groups of employees on a group basis. Private insurers then solicited business from companies who had pools of relatively healthy workers available to be insured. Because private insurers were for-profit, they were allowed to charge sicker pools of people higher premiums and healthier pools lower premiums.

The not-for-profit systems had to use a blended rating methodology for the entire community of those insured. This allowed private insurers to be more price-competitive and resulted in the significant growth of the numbers of Americans covered by private group plans.

As the market for health care insurance expanded from 21 million in 1940 to 63 million in 1950 all the way to 142 million by 1960, the door opened for private health care insurers, firmly establishing an employer-based mechanism as the primary means by which health care was accessed in the United States.

Government policies also supported the entrenchment of an employer-based system. The Wage Stabilization Act of 1942 limited employers from using wages as a means of competing for scarce labor, but allowed them to add insurance plans as a means of attracting and holding workers. Companies without health care plans were not competitive and would not be able to attract

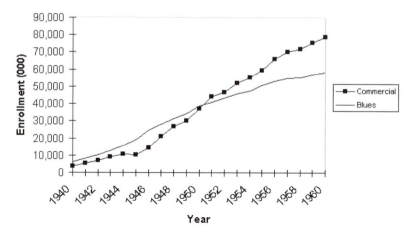

Figure 4.1 Enrollment in for-profit (commercial) and not-for-profit (blues) insurance programs, 1940–1960

workers. In the scheme of things, the plans were relatively inexpensive and a cost that all companies had to bear. The competitive playing field was level.

The employer-based approach to health care coverage was given another boost when in 1949 the National Labor Relations Board (NLRB) ruled that the term "wages" included pension and insurance benefits. Once coverage became a legitimate subject for labor negotiations, it was extended to management personnel and other white-collar nonunionized workers. There was an understandable reluctance by companies to concede that unions could negotiate a more attractive package of benefits for their members than a company was willing to give to those who did not belong to the union.

Finally, the AMA has consistently opposed nationalized health care coverage. The AMA imposed restrictions on physician supply while the demand for physician services skyrocketed, thereby providing income protection for AMA members. The AMA has effectively resisted any programs that would limit the ability of physicians to charge patients on the basis of ability to pay. Their fear has always been that a national system would impose fee limits. As a result, "the AMA played a significant role in defeating proposals for nationalized health insurance in 1930 (under the Social Security Act) and later in defeating the proposed Murray-Wagner-Dingell (MWD) Bill in 1949. The MWD bill would have provided comprehensive nationalized health insurance to all Americans."[15]

The problem with using an employer-based approach to health care coverage as the primary means of access was bought home to me during a recent visit to my physician. I learned that his lab technician did not have health insurance. My doctor, just as thousands of others do, controls his labor costs by using part-time temporary help who never reach the threshold of 1,560 hours per year necessary to qualify for benefit coverage. These health care workers have become among the masses of permanent part-time, temporary part-time, and independent contractors without coverage. And as health care becomes even more expensive, more companies (especially small ones) will likely decide that they cannot afford to offer it. So, one side of the problem is the large number of employees working for organizations that do not offer coverage. The other side has to do with companies deciding they can no longer afford the system. Between 1980 and 1990, per capita heath care spending rose 156 percent, and another 71.5 percent the following decade. Companies passed these increases on to their customers and/or absorbed them themselves. Now, however, "this time of intense competition and overcapacity in many industries has made it difficult for businesses to pass these cost increases along to their customers and clients. As a result, insurance premium costs are being shifted to employees to absorb."[16]

The context in which health care coverage exists has changed from being a benefit used to attract workers to a cost in need of control. As a cost, companies have several available strategies and can adopt any one or a combination of: absorbing the costs; passing them on to employees or customers; employing larger numbers of part-time workers who are not benefit-eligible; or shifting work offshore, out from under the American system all together.

Exactly which combinations will emerge is unclear. However, we do know that the percentage of people covered by their employer dropped to 60.4 percent in 2003, down from 61.3 percent the year before. A third of those not covered are reported to be in households with incomes of 50K a year or more.[17]

With no universal health care system in place, not having a job forces the would-be American worker into a game of roulette few are anxious to play. The admission ticket for getting coverage comes with having a good job. But the context in which having a good job exists has changed. These changes have brought with them an ever-expanding permission to do what is necessary to compete. As Jeffrey Garten, former dean of the Yale School of Management, has observed:

> Health care is the elephant in the closet. Because American companies are not going to be able to afford the rising cost of health care, they will hire people elsewhere where those cost aren't so great. . . . This was not the problem of other adjustment periods. So we are basically competing not just on innovation, but on the cost of our social choices. And I don't think we have begun to face that.[18]

It is not just about the math of the net impact of offshoring and outsourcing. It is about context and what we are giving employers permission to do. Does the country have an obligation to provide access to the health care? Can we cede that responsibility to employers who are more concerned about costs than health? The United States has chosen to have an employer-based system for gaining access to affordable health care. With that has come the unusual circumstance of a context that may be inadequate to meet our national purposes. An increasing number of Americans now appear job-locked, a term invented to denote people who would leave their current employer were it not for certain health care benefit coverage issues.

An equally dramatic shift has happened in health care retiree benefits. Health care coverage for retirees is one of the particularly attractive features of some pension plans. In a time when people are living longer and the last few years of life are virtually impossible to fund privately, retiree health care coverage is the ultimate safety net. The precipitous rise in retiree health care expenses was a cause for alarm because companies were incurring future liabilities unaccounted for in any of their financial statements. There was no way for the investor community or financial rating agencies to know the size of an organization's liabilities with regard to retiree health care. In response, the Financial Accounting Standards Board (FASB), a quasi-governmental oversight agency whose rulings have the weight of law, ruled that these liabilities had to be accounted for on the balance sheet. The impact was to make retiree health care an immediate issue and a benefit slated for elimination.

Access to the American health care insurance system is fundamentally contingent on having a good job. The availability of good jobs relies on the requirement that companies compete for American-based labor. It is assumed that employers will be compelled to offer employees a value proposition that includes health care insurance. There is also an assumption that the interest of employers perfectly coincides with that of the nation in providing access to health care. Neither assumption is standing the test of time. Once work becomes global, companies are compelled to follow global industry best practices in order to remain competitive. In many instances this could mean shedding themselves of costs its global competitors are not obliged to absorb. At this point, employee-funded benefits become reasonable targets for reduction and even elimination.

Now, as work spreads beyond national boundaries and companies are forced to compete on a more global basis, the interests of the corporation migrates toward even more efficient and less costly modes of production. This is increasingly at odds with providing access to an ever more expensive health care delivery system.

Are corporations greedy? If by greed one means they are anxious to provide better returns on capital, I suppose they are. But that is a requirement of a free enterprise system and hardly outside acceptable boundaries. The problem is not with corporate greed, but rather with what we have asked American-based companies to do. In the end it will be necessary to establish alternative ways to ration and pay for health care. If not, safety net erosion will likely continue and even accelerate.

PENSION COSTS

The same erosion is applicable to pensions. How Americans save for retirement has undergone a dramatic shift in terms of the numbers of households being covered by defined benefit (DB) plans as compared to those covered by defined contribution (DC) plans. A defined benefit plan is one in which "the benefit a worker is to receive upon retirement is determined by a formula based on earnings history and years of service." DC plans are ones in which the employer and employee both contribute to pay for the benefit when the employee retires, and the amount depends on how much of a defined contribution is in the account.[19] Three reasons are given for these changes, all having to do with corporate profitability. DC plans shift the risks to workers, eliminate long-term corporate pension liabilities, and companies generally lower their contribution costs. The benefits of DC plans are so attractive to employers that between 1983 and 1998 the number of workers in the age group 47–64 covered by them rose from 12 to 60 percent. During that same period the number of households covered by DB plans dropped 27 percentage points, from 69 to 42 percent.

What difference does this make? Just this: "Despite the proliferation of defined contribution plans at a time when the stock market experienced one of its longest bull runs in history, the wealth of middle-aged households did not improve. Despite the hype, the switchover from DB to DC plans has not benefited the average family—instead it has hurt the average family [and] . . . is part of the general unraveling of the worker safety net."[20]

This also happened at a time when companies, under the protection of bankruptcy laws, began asking to be relieved of their pension obligations. The Pension Benefit Guaranty Corporation, established in 1974, today insures 31,000 plans. The good news is 500,000 workers from 2,700 terminated plans have needed the insurance and got it. The bad news is the guarantees are paid out, in many instances, at much less than their full value. Therefore, retirees must adjust their retirement plans to accommodate lower than expected retirement incomes. But more than that, the ability to escape pension obligations creates an uneven playing field for others in the industry. It is as if the lack of a pension obligation becomes an industry best practice from the perspective of cost control.

COMPANY-SPONSORED CAREER DEVELOPMENT

Career development programs, just as with health care benefits and pensions, were initially designed to be a part of a comprehensive employee value proposition in which retention was a key factor. Peter Capelli, a professor at the Wharton School of Business, made the startling observation "that long-term, across the board employee loyalty is neither possible nor desirable." He pointed to Prudential "targeting" the people they want to retain and giving up on the notion that "employees are going to stay with one company for life." He discussed how UPS is identifying the skills they want to retain and, "for workers without them, allowing the revolving door to spin." He advises "once you know which employees you need to retain and, for how long, you can use a number of mechanisms to encourage them to stay. The key is to resist the temptation to use mechanisms across the board."[21]

These examples are a testimonial to the distance American industry has come in establishing new employee value propositions. The revolving door will likely apply to any set of workers where employee retention is more costly and less feasible than turnover. But the revolving door is more than a portal for jobs; it is the primary entry for access to a way life we have come to accept as a part of our birthright as Americans.

Are there any good jobs left? From a numbers standpoint, there is not enough global capacity to do all the jobs Americans do, and outsourcing and offshoring account for a small portion of the good jobs available. In addition, offshoring is not easy. It is so difficult that a new consulting niche has emerged in which companies are hired to teach the fine art of offshoring.

It is a good thing some good jobs are left, because we do not know how much longer that will be the case; and it gives us needed time to adjust—time perhaps for new public policies and individual strategies for survival. We need time to improve our collective and individual levels of understanding.

Thomas Friedman (*The World Is Flat*) speaks of visiting call-centers in India in which people are learning to speak English with an American accent.[22] We are still in a time in which English is one of the most important skills any global worker can have. It is not unreasonable to believe that very soon knowledge of Chinese will be equally as important, if not more so.

The choice facing those in transition or launching new careers is becoming bimodal. They can maintain their current mind-set and look for one of the good jobs that emerged out of the World War II time of plenty. These are available but increasingly difficult to find. The alternative is to change one's mind-set and begin functioning more fully in the global economy. Though difficult, it may be the only real alternative. People have not yet arrived at this conclusion. They will need to change their behaviors as well to reflect the thought processes that support them.

As this transition takes place, some readers will want to know how issues of race and gender will impact the career management process. However, as interest in this question is not universal, readers should feel free to skip the discussion in Chapter Five and move directly to Chapter Six which begins the discussion of "Practical Applications."

To others, there are at least four reasons why race and gender issues might be of interest and why further examination is an important component for understanding the context in which jobs exist today. The most obvious applies to females and minorities themselves who are aware their career chances have been affected by how these issues have historically played out. They may have a self-interested curiosity about how globalization will impact their situations in the years to come.

Improved conceptual clarification is another reason why someone would be interested. From the perspective of public policy, race and gender are sometimes seen as extensions of one another. After all, both involve issues of underrepresentation and access to opportunities that have traditionally been closed. However, understanding how they differ also facilitates a more complete understanding of how each is unique and why, at times, they require different public policy treatments.

There are also instances during the hiring process when minorities and women (also known as protected classes) are culled out for special attention. Companies will sometimes sponsor special sessions for these groups in an effort to demonstrate that the old rules of exclusion are no longer applicable. In hiring situations in which the supply of applicants exceeds the number of available jobs, these special sessions take on an air of favoritism (sometimes called reverse discrimination) and are a source of ill will.

Finally, the issue is important to the nation as a whole. As we shall argue, barriers to the freedoms people have to pursue ways of life they find valuable can be a major deterrent to a fuller utilization of individual capabilities. Barriers that keep people "un-free" are not only costly to them, but are also costly to the society as a whole. In this sense, the imposition of race and gender-based limitations is doubly taxing. Those interested in the ability of the United States to compete in a more global economy will also find the discussion of interest.

CHAPTER FIVE

☙❧

RACE AND GENDER IN THE JOB SEARCH PROCESS

RACE AND GENDER matter in American social and economic life. How they actually play out is less obvious than one would think. Minorities and women are concerned about how their careers and job search prospects are impacted. They wonder about how to deal with these factors and whether the day will come when race and gender will be less relevant.

Some white males may be confused by attention to these matters. They are constantly reminded that candidate slates are put together to show some measure of diversity. To them the very process of insisting that females and minorities be included on candidate slates diminishes the chances of their résumés being visible in a stack of applications that easily could number in the hundreds. Any consideration of credentials not directly related to the job at hand feels like reverse discrimination. They may see laws prohibiting discrimination and requiring affirmative action as marginalizing white male applicants. Discussions about adverse impact and diversity during hiring and termination processes appear as little more than code for "preferential treatment." On the other hand, minorities are unlikely to view diversity on candidate slates as progress unless it results in diversity in hires, promotions, and more general career opportunities.

These topics are emotionally charged and not easily discussed in mixed company, as all sides tend to see their points of view as self-evident truths.

I am reminded of a young man I know who was convinced that his opportunity to become a college head football coach was greatly and inappropriately diminished because of the requirements of affirmative action. According to him, he could not get a job because colleges were under pressure to hire African-Americans. He held to this view in spite of overwhelming statistical evidence to the contrary. In 2005, 50 percent of all football players at the 117 Division I-A participating schools were African-American. In contrast, 97 percent of all head coaches and 75 percent of all assistant coaches were white. These numbers meant nothing to our young man, partly because with each application and subsequent rejection the schools made sure he and others understood their institution's commitment to affirmative action. The posters in the hallways of the personnel office and the way newspaper ads were written were visible evidence that people were invited to apply regardless of race, color, creed, sex, national origin, or sexual orientation. In addition, the NCAA (the body of college and university presidents governing collegiate athletics) has been vocal about its intention to increase minority hiring among college and university athletic departments. In today's environment, white males have to compete against pools of applicants greatly expanded by the requirements of affirmative action.

Many women also believe that their career success is limited by considerations of gender in spite of some important evidence to the contrary. For example, in 2004, 49.6 percent of all students admitted to American medical schools were women. This was up from the 40 percent admitted in 1993 and is anticipated to go to 57 percent by 2020.[1] The acceptance of women in the medical profession has ebbed and flowed over the past hundred years. For a time after the Civil War the medical profession was open to women. But around the turn of the century, according to Paul Starr, the number of women entering the medical profession began a precipitous decline.

> It was first thought the declining numbers of women reflected declining demand for women doctors or declining interest among women in becoming physicians. Others, however, have since pointed out the active hostility of men in the profession. As places in medical school became more scarce, schools that previously had liberal policies toward women increasingly excluded them. Administrators justified outright discrimination against qualified women candidates on the grounds that they would not continue the practice after marriage. For the next half century after 1910, except for war time, the schools maintained quotas limiting women to about 5 percent of student admissions.[2]

But the numbers are confusing. By one measure women have made great strides as full participants in the workforce and now hold over half of all management and professional positions. By other measures they have a long way to go, especially when one considers that women are only 7.9 percent of *Fortune* 500 top earners, and that only 1.4 percent of *Fortune* 500 chief executive officers are women.

A wealth of conflicting information is available about the impact of race and gender, which contributes to the varying perceptions people have about these issues. The first step we shall take in eliminating the confusion is to separate the issues from one another. Recent history has encouraged a view of race and gender as being merely different sides of the same coin. Separating them will allow us to see each one more clearly in the context in which they have historically existed and how they differ from one another today. We bring them back together in the final chapter, because they will be similarly impacted by requirements in the new economy. Survival and prosperity will likely be less dependent on past prejudices and will be more a function of the ability any of us have to create value. The great leveling of the economic playing field will make hanging on to dysfunctional political agendas and beliefs more costly and less likely than ever before.

RACE IN AMERICA

To this point, we have used "minority" and "race" somewhat interchangeably. Continuing to do so would be a mistake. Many of the principles that apply to the status of any minority in a majority system are relevant across all minority groups. Minorities in American political and social life transform themselves into majorities by forming coalitions with other groups and being willing to compromise. Without belaboring the detail, this feature of the American political system has been a major source of its stability over time. Those outside the system can decide to become politically active and get at least some of what they want. In this sense American political life is a minimalist game, and the differences between political outcomes tend to be Tweedledee-Tweedledum.

The African-American experience is a significant exception. Though substantial social and economic progress has been made, poverty and urban ghettos persist, and being black in America still extracts a price over and above that of membership in other groups. More recent immigrants to America may not understand why these issues are still with us. To them, a better life may appear available for any who want it and are willing to sacrifice. They probably wonder if the issues are more a matter of personal character and not of ongoing structural barriers. This kind of explanation appeals to the "rugged individualism" on which the country was built and that took it from a noble experiment in democracy to a world power.

The response from many African-Americans to this view is often immediate and emotional. This is a point in time where some see progress and others see continued subjugation—where some see preferential treatment, others see justifiable efforts at inclusion. For some, the legal rights of African-Americans as citizens have long been settled. For others, danger lurks. How is it that different people come to such radically different conclusions when viewing the same objective reality? The answer is the key to understanding race in America, and race sets the outer limits for how minorities negotiate participation in the social and economic life of the country. It will also greatly influence how America comes to grips with the global leveling of the economic playing field.

Race in America is a complicated, emotional topic, difficult for people to discuss and understand. While losing one's job can be emotional, it is more easily discussed than race. Race is not a subject that strangers of different races discuss casually with one another just to pass time. This hypersensitivity has left the nation with a retarded sense of these issues along with a lack of historical perspective. What people understand of race is often limited to the latest sound bite from the news and their own narrow, personal experiences. They seem to know a little about affirmative action and reverse discrimination, but not much more. This truncated view allows the subject to be depicted as a struggle about integration. While there is some limited accuracy to this account, considerably more has historically been at stake.

It is true that from World War II forward, much of what showed up in the news focused on integration. The desegregation of the armed services under Truman; the 1954 Supreme Court decision mandating integration of the public schools; President Kennedy's Executive Order 11246 requiring government contractors to take affirmative action; and the 1964 Civil Rights Act, making certain types of discrimination illegal, all had heavy integrationists overtones. But the failure to look at post–World War II American race relations in a larger context misses the mark and confuses the casual observer. In truth, postwar developments in race relations were a continuation of more than 200 years of debate. The context of that debate and how it has evolved over time influences the path forward for minorities as they look for jobs and plan careers.

Context explains a lot. Consider for a moment the remarkable action taken by the United States Senate on June 13, 2005, approving a resolution apologizing for its failure to enact antilynching legislation over the past century or more.[3] The action was not widely anticipated in the popular press, and there was virtually no debate leading up to the Senate's action. How is it that a topic that so inflamed the passions of an entire nation a few short decades before could be addressed with little or no fanfare? The failure to make lynching a federal crime gave some license as individual citizens to carry out their own local brand of vigilante justice.

The resolution was met with a collective national yawn, as more pressing issues, such as the war in Iraq and jobs being lost to outsourcing, occupied the American conscience. Americans were perhaps uninterested because the resolution belabored the obvious. But it also may have signaled the beginning of the end to a long history of national denial. For our purposes, passing an antilynching resolution in the United States Senate by unanimous consent was evidence of an evolving context in which the country took a step toward putting race in its rearview mirror rather than keeping it as the deer in the headlights it had been for more than two centuries. The way the issue was initially framed and how it played out over time left the country with a perspective on questions of race that was difficult to overcome. It also provided the contemporary context in which America's racial and ethic minorities manage their careers and job transitions. That is, the perception that the general society has had of African-Americans is largely informed by a set of beliefs and attitudes that are integral components of a mind-set that was centuries in the making and is only recently beginning to be dismantled. Vestiges of those centuries remain.

Two factors in the debate about race made the path toward resolution different from most other issues. The first had to do with the status of slaves as property rather than people. Property owners in America have always had rights and privileges outlined in considerable detail in local, state, and national laws. Ending slavery meant those laws of property had to be totally redefined, requiring nothing less than constitutional amendments. The redefinition, in turn, never fully abandoned its view of Africans as objects of law for purposes of control rather than for freedom. Changing any aspect of the rights and privileges of African-Americans required wholesale changes across a broad swath of the nation. At every point then, the resolution of race in America consumed the entire nation. This accounts for the extended debate about states' rights and the authority of the federal government relative to the states.

The second factor has to do with the debate being one-sided. It was largely a debate among those of European descent about Africans, and informed by a Eurocentric view of the world. There was a close link between how the problem was perceived and the solutions that were proposed. For example, and on the slightly different subject of Native Americans, portraying the American West as "unsettled" gave post–Civil War expansion an air of legitimacy it might not otherwise have had. Settling the West was a polite way of saying the land was occupied by persons deemed otherwise unworthy. In this context, Americans were not stealing land, they were settling it.

Likewise, the debate about race was never about the character of Europeans. Rather, it was always about what Africans needed to do or become in order to be more palatable. The idea that the problem rested with the conquered and not the conquerors assumed the status of an a priori assumption whose truth was self-evident. That perspective did not just make it easy for Americans to hang on to stereotypic concepts about race, it required it. The way the debate has been shaped allowed vestiges of the racial thinking of the past to survive until today. In this context, racial progress was measured against less than fully meaningful standards. That is, what may have seemed like progress to those of European descent was really more of a one-sided measurement. From the perspective of others, there was little progress at all. The measurement of progress for many years was against how offended whites have been to be in the presence of African-Americans. Even today, movement along this continuum is measured and reported as relative progress. As we shall see a little later during our discussion of the integration of Major League Baseball, such measurements miss the point.

This is not a problem unique to Europeans or to discussions about race. It happens anytime knowledge about a given subject is informed by too narrow a perspective. It is a problem about the social context of knowledge and how to make it less dependent on the social space one occupies. In that sense, context dictates perception, and perception is everything. Those two realities—the necessity to define (control) the relationship of the black population to the more general society and embed that relationship into law, and the one-sided nature of the discussion—created a national ideology about race and a corresponding context for race relations in America that was difficult to overcome.

Discussions about progress or the lack thereof have likewise been retarded and viewed in much too narrow a context. The typology of freedoms offered by Amartya Sen in his book *Development as Freedom*,[4] is useful for purposes of expanding our understanding of race beyond the traditional American context. Sen offers five instrumental freedoms against which we can measure progress (development). These include:

> **Political Freedoms**, which we traditionally understand as civil rights and "refer to the opportunities that people have to determine who shall govern and on what principles."
>
> **Economic Facilities** "refer to the opportunities that individuals respectively enjoy to utilize economic resources for the purpose of consumption, production and exchange."
>
> **Social Opportunities** "refer to the arrangements that society makes for education, health care and so on which influence the individual's substantive freedom to live better."
>
> **Transparency** refers to the basic presumption that society operates at a basic level of trust and freedom so people can deal with one another under guarantees of disclosure and lucidity.
>
> **Protective Security** keeps people from the verge of vulnerability and from great deprivation as a result of changes that adversely affect their lives

According to Sen, these freedoms are interrelated and affect each other in terms of their mutual enhancement or deprivation. That is, denying any one of the five instrumental freedoms affects an individual's access to the others. This in turn can have a dramatic and precipitous impact on the ability of people to develop as full participants in a society. Being denied the basic social safety net of security of health care and premature morbidity keeps one from the effective utilization of other freedoms.

What are the implications for race in America? In order to provide greater clarity, it is helpful to examine four historic Supreme Court decisions (or touch-points) that represented major developments in race relations. Sen's typology allows us to examine each touch-point against the backdrop of its impact on the freedoms of African-Americans. This yardstick begins to provide a rough measure of progress toward freedom, racial equality, and the subsequent ability of African-Americans to become full partners in the life of the country. As we shall see, being promised equal protection by the Constitution is not sufficient without having the right to vote. Having the right to vote may mean little without adequate access to health care and other more general welfare opportunities experienced by the larger society. Even having access to health care is not fully sufficient without being free from premature morbidity.

Is it fair though to hold certain Supreme Court decisions accountable for accomplishing things they were never intended to accomplish? It is certainly not fair. But three of these decisions are often held up as examples of substantial progress for blacks in America. It is appropriate to ask what was accomplished. It becomes a question of results and not of intent.

The four decisions are: *Dred Scott v. Sanford, Plessy v. Ferguson, Gaines v. Canada,* and *Brown v. Board of Education of Topeka, Kansas.* We have perhaps too easily forgotten the arrogance and harshness of the issues. The discussions were about Africans as property rather than people; their inclination or not toward criminal behavior; if they are morally and socially inferior; should they be sent back to Africa, or be kept separate from whites; and, whatever else anyone's imagination could concoct.

Some of those thoughts, though thankfully not all, are still with us and form the context in which race plays out. Other immigrants faced similar stereotypic brandings, but they did not persist from one generation to the next as easily as those involving race. The accommodation of the Italians or Irish may have been difficult for selected cities like Boston or New York, but they never were the concern for the entire nation all at once and never subjected to the perceived need to be redefined as people rather than property. These fundamental changes in the social structure of the American society help create an unparalleled and persistent hysteria about race. For most of the history of the nation, the majority population was allowed to hang on to whatever answers they had concocted for themselves about the character and destiny of Africans. For many, though, it was more than permission, it was a requirement.

Dred Scott v. Sanford (1856).[5] Choosing Dred Scott as one of the touchpoint decisions of the legal embodiment of racial prejudice requires justification. After all, it has been referred to as one of the most overturned Supreme Court decisions in history. As pointed out by Don Fehrenbacher in his book *The Dred Scott Decision,* "The Thirteenth Amendment ratified late in 1865 made the decision rendered by Chief Justice Taney obsolete."[6] This decision, like so many others that went before and came after, essentially left the basic assumptions of the differences between the races intact. As a result, it left in place a body of racial ideology that served as a particular style of thought informing the worldview of the white majority. Racial inferiority of nonwhites was assumed to be true and an appropriate cornerstone in the law of the land. The only question was whether this presumed inferiority meant that nonwhites had to be accorded equal protection under the law.

The so-called problem of the Negro was for most of the past 200 years dominated by a concern about the conditions under which whites could tolerate the presence of another race. Each of the touch-points since Dred Scott has been portrayed as a key event in the march toward equality. But by leaving the body of racist ideology intact, the progress was more apparent than real.

The basic facts of the case are that Dred Scott was a slave in the State of Missouri who had traveled *to* other freehold states in the company of his owner. Missouri law had been clear that slaves residing in free territories *or* states for an extended period were considered emancipated. In and of itself, the Scott case did not contain significantly new or different legal issues. What makes it of interest here is the majority opinion authored by pro-slavery advocate Chief Justice Taney. He took this opportunity to speak to the whole range of issues regarding what he saw as the Negro problem. To this extent, it represents a stake in the ground from which deviation can be measured. It provides a concise sense of what the issues were and how they were resolved within the context of a Eurocentric worldview that unquestionably accepted its own superiority. Progress toward a more egalitarian society is made only when the underlying assumptions of racial superiority are questioned in support of a mind-shift and different worldview.

That shift began to happen just recently. Between then and now, the discussion has been about how the shift will play out in the everyday lives of citizens. Meanwhile, we are still left with a residue of thought about race that continues as a part of the American mind.

Two central assertions in the Dred Scott case stand out for attention: the question of association with whites, and what obligation was owed to blacks with regard to rights. Taney argued that "[the black race] had for more than a century before been regarded as being of an inferior order, and altogether unfit to associate with the white race [and] had no rights which the white man was bound to respect."[7] To Taney, people of African descent were never intended to be citizens, and even when granted citizenship they could in turn be reduced to slavery if the voters of any of the several states so wished.

Taney's opinion was issued on the eve of the Civil War and laid out the issues the nation would struggle with for over a century. Being unfit to associate with whites and not having rights that others were obliged to respect were basic belief patterns that persisted and were partially embedded in the law. After the war, states passed a myriad of laws prescribing the circumstances under which the races could coexist. These overwhelmingly enforced rigid standards of racial separation, which allowed the worldview of the majority to essentially survive unchallenged.

The view of the vast majority of white Americans before the Civil War and after was that Africans were not in any way their equal and had no rights anyone was obliged to recognize. The impact of so many people holding this view is easy to anticipate. None of the five freedoms were available to any great extent to any American of African descent. Looking at it from the perspective of development as freedom, the end of slavery did not result in the ability of blacks to pursue ways of life they found of value. They were, in Sen's terms, unfree; and the Civil War did not change that.

Plessy v. Ferguson (1896).[8] Post-Reconstruction America was a period in which greater definition was given to the way the races would be allowed to coexist. With the issue of citizenship resolved, the question now was what kinds of citizens those of African descent were allowed to be. This led to a seemingly endless discussion about the definition of race. When are people considered members of one race versus another when they are of mixed lineage? Wherever that line was drawn in the various states, the races were required to be separate but equal. In truth, they were separate and unequal. That is, based on American racial ideology, those of African descent were still deemed unfit to associate with whites. In some respects the ruling in *Plessy* is less important than what it demonstrated. White America was obsessively occupied with questions of race.

The facts of the case are that Homer Plessy, described as one-eighth Negro and seven-eighths white, was denied access to the whites-only railcar. There is some evidence that the entire case was contrived given that Plessy went out of his way to bring the matter to the attention of a porter in order to get himself arrested. He sued on grounds that he was not a member of the Negro race either by appearance or blood. The objective seems to have been to point up the absurdity of race-based distinctions with regard to public accommodations. The Supreme Court's interest in the case turned on Plessy's argument that Louisiana law requiring separate but equal public accommodations was a denial of equal protection under the Thirteenth and Fourteenth Amendments to the Constitution. The punch line was: Separate but equal was upheld as constitutional. But looking closer at the law, one can see how far it went to prescribe how whites and blacks were to relate to one another.

The law first stipulated that "no persons shall be allowed to occupy seats in coaches other than the ones assigned to them on account of the race they belong to." Any passenger in violation or any official failing to enforce it were subject to a $25 fine or twenty days in jail. Nurses attending to children were exempted.

Such detail is typical of the systematic patchwork of laws that dominated American jurisprudence and thought for centuries. Even the Supreme Court found it appropriate to weigh in on the question of who was white and who was not: "It is true that the question of the proportion of colored blood necessary to constitute a colored person, as distinguished from a white person, is one upon which there is a difference of opinion in the different states; some holding that any visible admixture of black blood stamps the person as belonging to the colored race (*State v. Chavers*, 5 Jones); others, that it depends upon the preponderance of blood (*Gray v. State*, 4 Ohio, 354; *Monroe v. Collins*, 17 Ohio St. 665); and still others, that the predominance of white blood must be in the proportion of three-fourths (*People v. Dean*, 14 Mich. 406; *Jones v. Com.*, 80 Va. 544), but these are questions to be determined under the laws of each state, and are not properly put in issue in this case. Under the allegations of this petition, it may undoubtedly become a question of importance whether, under the laws of Louisiana, the petitioner belongs to the white or colored race."[9]

Continued local enforcement and failure to reconcile divergent views of race left a residue of racist thought and ideology to stand in support of whatever local agenda might exist at the time. The Plessy decision further embedded separate-but-equal into law and legitimated its application across the full spectrum of the social and political life of the nation. It gave senators, congressmen, and everyday citizens the ammunition they needed to enforce rigid patterns of separation. It was a separation that often took pernicious forms. During Reconstruction, students at the traditionally black colleges were asked not to carry books from one class to the next for fear that white benefactors would conclude they were learning things inappropriate to people of African descent (a clear denial of freedom and the ability to develop).

Enforcing segregation became every white man's burden. In this context, lynching was not simply tolerated, it was encouraged. Few thought that Sen. James Heflin (D-AL) was speaking in the extreme in 1930 when he said "whenever a Negro crosses this dread line between the white and Negro races and lays his black hand on a white woman, he deserves to die."[10] This was the same thought pattern and code that years later precipitated the murder of Emit Till and allowed its perpetrators to go unpunished in spite of overwhelming evidence of their guilt.

Between 1882 and 1968, more than 4,700 people—most of them black males—were lynched. During this time, and in spite of the requirements of equal protection, the United States Senate was unable to muster enough support to make lynching a federal crime. It is as if the white majority knew that racial separation, control over education, and unrestricted vigilantism were key mechanisms of control and subjugation.

Vernon Jordan, former head of the Urban League, recalled his own personal encounter with attitudes of segregationists when he was home from college and working as a domestic in the home of Robert Maddox. Maddox discovered the young Mr. Jordan reading a book from his library and was dismayed to find out that Vernon could read. During their ensuing conversation, Maddox learned that Jordan was attending college at DePauw University and studying to become a lawyer. That evening, Maddox summoned his family's attention at the dinner table and said:

> I have an announcement to make. Vernon can read. And he is going to school with white children. No one made a sound. Finally, with great emotion, Maddox said. "I knew all of this was coming. But I'm glad I won't be here when it does."[11]

This happened to Jordan in the summer of 1955 and was a consistent component of an entire pattern of thought regarding race in America. While much has happened between then and now, it is unrealistic to think so much has changed that the impact of race has been eliminated. An examination of the next two touch-points will assist us in understanding what remains.

Gaines v. Canada (1938).[12] The significance of *Gaines v. Canada* lies with what it made painfully clear: Only the "separate" in the separate-but-equal doctrine appeared connected to public policy and social practice. Lloyd Gaines was refused admission to the School of Law at the University of Missouri on the grounds of separate-but-equal. The state had made provision "for the attendance of Negro residents of the state of Missouri at the University of any Adjacent State."[13] The Court ruled in essence, that Gaines was denied admission based on Missouri's requirement of separation, but state laws had not mandated the establishment of an equal facility and was, therefore, in violation of the requirements outlined in *Plessy v. Ferguson.*

Lest some think that these were or are academic questions without consequence, Gaines never attended the University of Missouri and was never heard from again. It is generally presumed that he was murdered rather than be allowed to be educated with whites. The ruling did not invalidate separate-but-equal as the law of the land. It was an affirmation that the equal part of the requirement needed to be taken more seriously. Again, much of the racist ideology and thought of the time mandating separation of the races continued to exist unchallenged. And though the ruling in *Gaines* was an undeniable step forward, it was not the leap the country needed to release the forces of freedom from the perspective of a more complete opportunity for development.

Brown et al. v. The Board of Education of Topeka, Kansas (1954).[14] The Brown case marked the beginning of the end of a racial ideology built over three centuries of political thought and social practice. The ruling had many interesting turns, but for our purposes it is sufficient to know that separate-but-equal was determined to be inherently unequal. The majority opinion was delivered by Chief Justice Earl Warren, an Eisenhower appointee who a few years earlier had been governor of California—a post he rose to on the back of his support for the internment of 110,000 Japanese-Americans as "enemy aliens" during World War II. He later revoked his views and apologized for having been part of an ignoble history.

The Supreme Court advised the nation to enforce its new dictum "with all deliberate speed." This has left some historians to observe that the emphasis in America since then has been more on the "deliberate" aspect in the ruling rather than the "speed." Clearly, though, Brown had implications beyond education. It meant, among other things the dismantling of an entire way of life and the reversal of an ideology of race. Just as Louisiana law in *Plessy v. Ferguson* was typical of the prescriptions used to separate the races, the Court's new ruling in *Brown* required enabling legislation to prescribe the details of what it meant in everyday life. Those prescriptions had actually started before *Brown* when Truman desegregated the armed services. After *Brown*, dramatic actions were required, beginning with the sending of federal troops into Little Rock, Arkansas, to quell local resistance to desegregation. In the main, the post-*Brown* actions were a negotiation of new terms under which the races would relate to one another. President Kennedy forced the issue by requiring government contractors to take affirmative action beginning in 1962. Under President Johnson's leadership, the 1964 Civil Rights Act prohibited certain kinds of discrimination, which for most of the history of the American republic were not only legal but also looked upon as acts of good citizenship. It is out of that powerful context that race is a consideration today. Vestiges of the racist ideology persist, as it is unreasonable to think they would disappear entirely in so short a time after centuries of incubation and manifestation in the collective mind of the nation.

The postwar demand for white-collar workers in conjunction with the GI Bill of Rights sent college enrollments soaring. It has been estimated that in 1947, ex-GIs made up 49 percent of the college population in the United States. While the 1930 U.S. population had doubled, college enrollment increased sevenfold between 1930 and 1950. But it was not until the 1960s that higher education opened its doors more widely to African-Americans.[15]

After World War II the GI Bill provided support to large numbers of men, and some women, from diverse backgrounds. However, it was not until the 1960s, thirty years after the feminization of campuses, that the number and percentage of African-Americans, the second wave of ethnic diversity, increased significantly. Responding to the civil rights movement, higher education opened its doors wider.

Were it not for the enabling action following *Brown*, it is fair to suggest that African-Americans would have missed the most rapid economic and educational expansion in American history. Black enrollment in higher education went from 274,000 (4.8 percent) in 1965 to over 1,100,000 (9.2 percent) in 1980.[16]

The world is getting flatter at a time when America is still in an era of among the firsts. During such a time it is possible to pass failure off as progress. Consider the occasion of Jackie Robinson as the first person of African-American descent to integrate Major League Baseball in 1946. That event is hailed nationally as being significant and positive, and signaled what was to come in the larger society. However, when contrasted against the integration of other sports leagues, it comes across also as a form of exploitation.

The Negro Leagues were viable economic entities filled with talented ballplayers. Under what other circumstance would it be a victory to move in and take the most talented players away with no compensation to the to league or team owners? Beyond that, the integration of baseball destroyed the infrastructure of the Negro leagues. Opportunities for black managers, owners, and other league officials were nonexistent. Contrast that to the acquisition of the American Football League (AFL) by the National Football League (NFL). Owners, managers, and league officials were either given opportunities in the new league or compensated as required. Americans seem to understand the appropriateness of compensation in one instance, but have generally not given a moment's thought to compensation in the other. That is because the movement toward social justice has been pitched as a struggle for integration rather than as one of development. And one way to measure development is to measure progress toward the five instrumental freedoms identified in *Development as Freedom*. Accepting the physical presence of one or two blacks among the white population is not necessarily progress.

Companies need to give the appearance of being inclusive. They often do this by creating prima facie evidence of having provided equal opportunity to classes of people that have traditionally been excluded. This creates ill will for all groups. Women and minorities suspect that the old practices of exclusion still apply, but they want to be hired and/or promoted based on their qualifications. White males wonder where their affirmative action program is. The position the country is in relative to race still has a long way to go. But where we are is undeniably better than where we were. The path forward will be affected by the leveling of the economic playing field.

Given the history of race ideology in America, as long as significant achievements place blacks in the category of "among the first of their race to do something," it is reasonable to assume that the ideology of race has not completely loosened its grip. Only when the coming and going of minorities in key positions of authority or accomplishments is the norm will we begin an exit. Until then, appointments like those of Richard Parsons, an African-American selected to be CEO of Time Warner, will be characterized as concessions to affirmative action. The difference it makes is in the minds of those making hiring or other selection decisions, who are not quite sure how to measure competence or predict success and have to rely on old patterns of behavior and worldviews for guidance. It is a mind-set that over 200 years has defined the problem as being one of race-based capability and capacity. Many of African-American descent understand the difficulty the United States Senate had in passing antilynching legislation. They tend not to understand, after more than two centuries of brutality and degradation at the hands of a population obsessed with race, why efforts to include them in the economic life of the nation can so easily be branded as reverse discrimination. Understandably, such characterizations have the feel of what has gone before. In light of the flattening of the economic playing field, it is a disposition that cannot be maintained. What takes its place are the grounds on which economic competition will continue.

GENDER

It is important to know that women's rights in America had its own history that at different points in time was extended to include issues of race. But for the most part, the two political movements were separate. How they came together in the formation of the 1964 Civil Rights Act provides context to the way in which gender continues as a relevant consideration.

Ever since passage of the Thirteenth and Fourteenth Amendments to the American Constitution immediately following the Civil War, the idea of giving people equal protection under the law regardless of race, color, or creed became standard language in American jurisprudence. And, ever since the 1964 Civil Rights Act was passed (specifically Title VII), sex was included in the mix of protections. They are often discussed as if they have always been considered in the same context. In truth, they were (and are) very different, though no less important to America's future. One important difference between the two is that the politics of race was overwhelmingly about the accommodation of a largely alien population brought to North America against its will. In contrast, discrimination on the basis of sex was about the legitimacy and prescription of gender-based social roles. It was about fathers, husbands, and sons juxtaposed to mothers, wives, and daughters.

Though there is some dispute about how sex got added to the list of protected classes in the 1964 Civil Rights Act, it is generally agreed to have been part of an ongoing compromise between two competing women's groups, the National Committee on the Status of Women (NCW) and the National Women's Party (NWP). The NWP was an offshoot of the women's suffrage movement and a strong advocate of the Equal Rights Amendment (ERA) to the Constitution—an amendment that would have given women and men equal status before the law. The ERA has been a part of the American lexicon for so many years, some may believe it has already been passed. It has not. The division among American women as to the need for such an amendment stands in stark contrast to the comparative unanimity among African-Americans about their equal rights in America and the associated remedies.

While both the NWP and NCW agreed that there was discrimination against women, the NCW was adamantly opposed to the ERA. Beginning in the 1940s, it adopted a more restrictive position in favor of "specific bills for specific ills" rather than the wide-ranging changes that would surely be ushered in by an ERA.

Prior to 1964 there was a patchwork of protective legislation in place that, among other things, limited the number of hours women could work, limited the number of pounds they could lift, prohibited night work; and identified occupations considered too dangerous for women. Whether this legal recognition of gender-based differences was tantamount to protection, suppression, or both, has been a source of disagreement among American women for well over a century and has been an insurmountable barrier to passage of the ERA. It has also served as the conceptual host for other issues of critical importance. These include whether or not there really is a gender gap, and whether the career penalties women bear when they choose to become mothers is gender-based discrimination or the appropriate outcome of personal choices. When examined closely, the politics of race and gender differ significantly.

The division among women on the politics of gender reflects a fundamental ambivalence that women themselves have about their careers and about gender-based roles in society. This division and its impact on the push for passage of the ERA were chronicled by Ann Crittenden in her book *The Price of Motherhood*. She noted:

> At the turn of the century, the women's movement contained two contradictory strands: one that denigrated women's role within the family and one that demanded recognition and remuneration for it. The first argued that only one road could lead to female emancipation and it pointed straight out of the house toward the world of paid work. The second sought equality for women within the family as well and challenged the idea that a wife and mother was the economic dependent of her husband.
>
> For the rest of the century, the women's movement followed the first path, and it led to innumerable victories. But in choosing that path, many women's advocates accepted the continued devaluation of motherhood, thereby guaranteeing that feminism would not resonate with millions of wives and mothers.[17]

Does gender still matter? The answer is that gender, like race, continues to be an important consideration. Exactly how it plays out, however, is anything but obvious. Furthermore, even though remedies against gender-based discrimination are housed in the same legislation for those involving race, they are not the same. Not surprisingly, however, the flattening of the world's economy will likely reduce the importance of both in determining one's ability to earn a living.

As some companies have discovered, continuing past practices of discrimination on the basis of gender can be expensive both in terms of punitive damage awards as well as brand image. Companies and institutions that rely on female customers are loath to have their brands compromised by accusations of sex discrimination. Even though the 1964 Civil Rights Act ushered in dramatic changes in the legal status of women, there are still unanswered questions about whether differences between men and women constitute discrimination. Many companies are appropriately aggressive when they have opportunities to create prima facie cases about their own diversity. The interviewing and hiring processes are the handiest targets for both guarding against discrimination and simultaneously demonstrating that it exists. Discrimination in hiring, promotion, and termination practices is seen as a first line of attack in Title VII charges. One of the first questions companies face is whether their pools of candidates have appropriate levels of diversity. Accommodating this requirement has necessitated more exacting definitions of job-related criteria, giving rise to the development of selection criteria and methodologies that dramatically improved selection processes.

At one time women could routinely and legally be eliminated from consideration for employment because they were not heads of households—or would probably not stay in the workforce when they bore children, were not strong enough to do the job, or did fit in well with the prevailing culture. As with race, an entire body of thought was developed to justify existing practices.

The social fabric holding beliefs in place created a powerful context for what people believed.

The once-legal differences in the treatment of women in the workplace and their inevitable consequences for wage differentials became known as the gender gap. Whether such a gap exists depends not only on who one asks, but also on how the term is defined. Three categories of inquiry are used here to guide our discussion. They include educational choices by gender, income levels of men and women, and traditional work-life balance issues.

Since World War II and the growth of the white-collar workforce, getting a college degree emerged as the primary means by which the American Dream has been pursued. The good jobs go disproportionately to those with post-secondary degrees. For sure, any hope of discovering and then closing income gaps between men and women would start with differential rates of access to higher education. Looking at the gender gap from this perspective reveals just how much of an impact antidiscrimination legislation has had. In a report prepared for the Business Roundtable (a nonpartisan not-for-profit interest group), in May 2003, it was reported that "as recently as 1977, women were awarded fewer college degrees than men. During the 1976–77 academic year

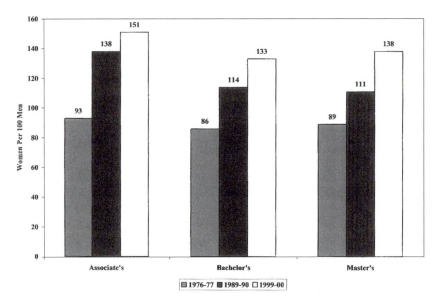

Figure 5.1 Trends in the number of associate, bachelor, and master's degrees awarded to women per 100 men.
Source: U.S. Department of Education, National Center for Education Statistics, Earned Degrees Conferred; Higher Education General Information Survey (HEGIS), "Degrees and Other Formal Awards Conferred" surveys; and Integrated Postsecondary Education Data System (IPEDS), "Completions" surveys; tabulations by authors.

more college degrees were conferred on men at every educational level. By the middle of the 1980s women were forging ahead of men in associate, bachelors and masters degrees awarded."[18]

The authors went on to observe that the gap in PhDs and professional degrees was closing fast, and that by 2009 would be 91 and 77 of every 100 degrees awarded to men, respectively.

The question then turns to whether women are pursuing degrees in the sciences and in engineering because that is where the future job creation and higher pay levels are. According to a report in the *Journal of Minerals, Metals and Materials (JOM)*, the number of degrees awarded to women from 1966 to 2001 in science and engineering has risen steadily to where it was equal to and slightly ahead of those awarded to men.

The same levels of enrollment for women are being reported in schools of medicine and law, where they are now 50 percent of the student population. The evidence is substantial. Enrollment and degree attainment of women has risen dramatically to the point of parity or its close approximation.

However, according an article in the December 1, 2004, issue of *Business Week*, female enrollment in the top thirty MBA programs continues to lag, with women making up on average only 30 percent for most schools. Several factors were identified as having a retarding effect on female enrollment,

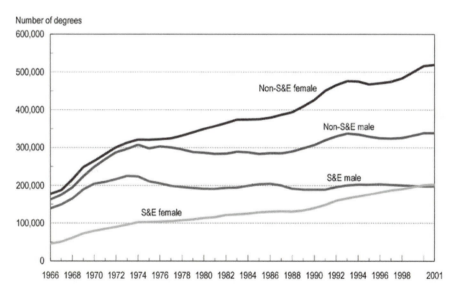

Figure 5.2 Number of college degrees awarded in science and engineering by male and female, 1966–2001.
Source: Women, Minorities, and Persons with Disabilities in Science and Engineering, 2004.

including the lack of role models, career risk tolerance of women versus men, gender stereotyping, curriculum, and timing. This last issue, timing, provides the greatest insight into a significant gender gap. "A major reason, some experts say, why women choose medical or law school over MBAs is that students can attend those directly out of undergraduate school. Most top MBA programs require at least three to five years of work experience. That's about the point in their lives when many women are planning to start a family and feel forced to choose between that and a career."[19]

One would think that measuring pay would be as straightforward as college enrollments. It is not. And that fact is a major source of the ongoing debate over the gender gap. According to a U.S. Census Bureau report, women earned seventy-six cents on the dollar as compared with their male counterparts.[20] The median income for men versus women was $40,668 and $30,724 respectively. Critics, however, are quick to point out that these figures do not take into consideration the voluntary decision women make to work part-time. When this is done, the gap narrows to twenty cents on the dollar.

It is a disparity that continues even at the higher levels of incomes. Female engineers were reported as making a full $17,000 a year less than their male counterparts in recent years. So even controlling for education, the gender gap appears alive and well. The matter does not end there. Other studies, like the one reported in the April 7, 2003, issue of *Chemical & Engineering News,*[21] control for age on the premise that younger women more closely approximate their male counterparts in education and experience. When that study looked at women chemists over and under the age forty, another set of patterns emerged.

- 75 percent of women chemists under age forty reported being satisfied with their current positions and careers, compared with 78 percent of the men.
- The gender gap in management has largely closed, with 5 percent of the women and 6 percent of men in management positions.
- Men and women working full-time tend to have equal salaries, with any gap being explained by educational differences.
- 11 percent of all chemists under forty experienced a career break of at least six months. The proportion of men and women who said the break did not negatively impact their careers was almost even.

According to William Ferrell (*Why Men Earn More*),[22] a significant portion of the gender gap can be explained by the different career choices women make. That is, women in positions dominated by females are paid less. When they make alternative career choices and opt for positions historically dominated by men, their incomes increase significantly. In some cases the gender gap virtually disappears. It is fair to say that gaps created by legal discrimination prior to 1964 have begun to close significantly. But it is unrealistic to think that gender-based barriers have been completely eliminated.

Assuming the role of primary caregiver and mother persists for women even when they work outside the home. Women with children tend to have two jobs— one at work outside the home and another providing the primary care for their children, even in the presence of fully engaged traditional husbands. This reality is well chronicled. Ann Crittenden has observed, "The care of babies and tod- dlers is still clearly a female monopoly. In families with pre-school children, mothers appear to be putting in roughly three to four times as many hours as fathers."[23] The rigidity of the female role as the primary caregiver for children continues to have significant career consequences. First, men with children have careers that are largely unaffected because their spouses assume the role of primary caregiver. In contrast, as women are unwilling and/or unable to shift their caregiving role in the family, they are much more likely than men to request part-time work or drop out of the workforce altogether. There is virtually no argument that the presence of children creates a gender gap both in annual earnings and in earnings over the course of an entire career. Men earn more than women because women with children prefer or are forced to work part-time.

Two full-time jobs are one too many for most people to handle for an extended period of time. Career earnings are also less for these women be- cause taking time off deals a blow to career advancement from which full recovery is difficult. There is an undeniable price of motherhood. The debate heats up at this point. Is this reality the result of inappropriate discrimination against women or the consequence of personal choices people are free to make or not make?

Some countries have moved forward in recognizing the special realities women encounter as primary caregivers. In France, for example, "every French mother, rich or poor, married or single, receives not only free health care but a cash allowance for each child." This makes it easier for women to remain as active members of the workforce outside the home. In Sweden women are eligible for paid leave of a year after childbirth, the opportunity to work fewer than eight hours a day, and a government stipend to help pay child care expenses.[24]

American-based institutions are beginning to make modest adjustments in operating procedures to accommodate the realities women face. Universities, for example, have begun to change the time frame for achieving tenure. Generally the first seven years of faculty life is spent doing intensive research and writing, after which tenure is either granted or denied. At the University of Washington, for example, a nontenured faculty member can request a tenure clock extension of up to a year for the birth of a child. In 2001 the American Association of University Professors (AAUP) recommended that institutions allow for a tenure clock stoppage for up to one year with the birth of each child.[25]

Many of the most prestigious law firms are following a similar tack. They recognize that the process of becoming an equity partner for women with children is difficult. Men and women drop out of large law firms at the same rate. What is different, according to an article in the March 19, 2006, edition of the *International Herald Tribune,* is that only 17 percent of the women in the top law firms are partners.[26] In response, lifestyle firms have emerged in an effort to make the path toward partner more navigable for men and women alike. Some firms have established a two-tiered salary structure in which working 1,800 billable hours per year is permitted at a given salary level. Those working 1,950 billable hours or more are eligible for as much as $15,000 in additional deferred income.

The general sense is that none of these adjustments has significantly reduced the incompatibility of conventional career patterns with motherhood. Beyond that, there are some who argue that they not only have not reduced it, but they should not. This view flies in the face of a substantial number of professional women who believe they are inappropriately forced to choose between their careers and the mommy track. A recent survey conducted by the Defense Research Institute and reported in the October 14, 2005, issue of the *ABA Journal* drove the point home in dramatic style. One survey respondent observed that "after returning from maternity leave some partners treated her as if her career had been tossed out with the placenta." Sixty-five percent of the women surveyed believed there was a glass ceiling, and 61 percent had considered leaving law altogether because of issues related to their gender.[27]

The role of women in America is undeniably constrained by the requirements of motherhood. Motherhood in the larger society has created a backdrop against which women compete for jobs. When they work in the home as unpaid laborers, three dominant questions are at issue: Do they create value; how is it measured; and who owns it?

At critical points in time over the past several hundred years, the work women have done in the home has been systematically devalued, so much so that by 1900 "wives and daughters without paying jobs were officially classified by the U.S. Bureau of the Census as dependents." That is, they were not recognized as creating measurable value (wages) to the household. This was exacerbated by the creation of the Gross National Product (GNP) as a measure of the value of goods and services sold—a measure with clear limitations, warned its creator, because it did not "measure intangibles such as improvements in a surgical technique, the value of clean water, or the care provided by a family member."[28] These definitions and worldviews are of substantial consequence. Consider the example of a divorced woman trying to lay claim to value created during the course of a marriage. The inability to successfully quantify and reclaim that value is a significant source of poverty for women and children from divorced families.

In the broader sense, using professionally trained women as unpaid laborers in the home whose value is not recognized is an expensive use of resources. At a time when the leveling of the economic playing field requires an "all hands on deck" mentality, the United States may be stuck with a debate about the role of women it cannot afford. As the world continues to flatten, Americans may choose to revisit the present laissez-faire approach about work among women of childbearing age. The same is true with reference to race. Continuing discussions about reverse discrimination and the use of quotas at the expense of a national effort to mobilize and engage all members of society to their fullest potential may be a discussion difficult to understand.

Many of these issues fall within the realm of public policy and collective action. But none of us are in a position to wait for them to be resolved. As it currently stands, our social choices have been largely relegated to individual organizations and institutions. Their collective and individual perceptions of what they can afford, what risks they should take, and their most immediate self-interest drives how each of us will seek to care for our families and ourselves. It is a delegation that works when the self-interests of our institutions coincide with those of the more general society. During these times, we are likely to believe that what is good for them is good for us. But what happens when the self-interests of the institutions shaping our social choices expand beyond our national boundaries? When Manpower, Wal-Mart, or GM no longer need to fund pensions and health care to attract American workers, how will these things be provided?

No doubt, our choices will continue to be refined through the workings of the political system. In the meanwhile, though, people need to search for jobs and plan careers. How they do this must take the employment value propositions companies are offering into consideration. Sometimes these propositions will contain elements of the good jobs we once knew; at other times they will not. Sometimes employers will appear motivated by employee-friendly policies; at other times they will seem not to care. At all times, however, companies will be what they have always been, self-interested economic entities determined to survive. Survival will require them to provide goods and services in some combination of quality and cost better than their competition. That is the context in which jobs exist today. How well any of us are treated will be, as it always has been, contingent on the perceived value we create. Immediately following World War II, a college degree was the passport to the perception of being able to create value and land a good job. Perhaps for the first time in modern history, value creation has to be more real than apparent. Where one went to school will be less important than what that employee brings to the table. We are entering an age in which we can no longer afford our prejudices. Skin color and gender are being trumped by value creation. How that plays out and its practical applications is what the balance of this book is about.

Beginning with Chapter Six, we turn our attention to some of the practical applications of the principles discussed so far. For now, how we go about planning careers and looking for work is influenced by the global economy not necessarily dominated by it. If trends hold, that will soon change.

PART II

❧❧

*Practical Applications**

° For additional support with the job search process visit www.rwilliamhollandconsulting
.com.

CHAPTER SIX

❧❧

RÉSUMÉS: PASSION, PARADOX, AND ETHICS

IT IS JUST before the start of the second session of Mary Parsons's networking group. She continues to call it "networking," though unsure of the continuing relevance this term has in the context of today's evolving workplace. A number of her clients are uncomfortable actually doing networking and are confused about how it works in the job search process. They wonder why Mary counsels them to avoid asking networking contacts about possible job openings. After all, their unemployment status is the obvious elephant in the room. Mary is nagged by a growing suspicion that networking, along with many other career transition methodologies, needs updating. She has made adjustments from time to time, but is concerned that more is required.

It has been only a couple of days since the group last met. Two meetings in such close proximity are unusual. Time between meetings gives those in transition a chance to integrate feedback on their elevator speeches and complete several online career planning exercises. A polished elevator speech is important because it helps one explain their situation to others in a relaxed and efficient way. This shows respect for the listener's time and helps in resisting the temptation to provide more detail than anyone needs or might be interested in knowing.

PASSION

The career planning exercises also serve an important function. Career choices are often a result of a confluence of circumstances rather than of conscious planning. Transition allows time for reflection. One of the favorite questions career counselors encourage clients to contemplate has to do with passion. "Are you passionate about what you do? If not, now may be a good time to change careers."

Passion is one of those overworked and misunderstood clichés that is seemingly a part of every counselor's tool kit. Developing the requisite skills for a career may not have much to do with passion. In fact, just the opposite is true.

Athletes understand this better than most. Their passion is about winning. The process of getting into the winner's circle involves repetition to the point of boredom. When athletes lose their appetite (passion) for competition, they sometimes exit the competitive arena by announcing they have lost their passion for the game. This apparently confuses some career counselors. Great athletes report that they spend many more hours practicing rather than playing. They distinguish the process from the prize and are not deterred when the process by itself fails to excite their passion. Passion can be important, but it is not the lead variable. So making career choices by prematurely focusing on passion can too easily beg the wrong question. One virtue of Bolles's work in *Parachute* is his advice to people thinking about career choices to figure out what they are good at rather than passionate about.

We have come a long way from the days when Humble Oil tried to find work for its excess white-collar workers. If finding another job was easy then, it is not as easy now. And people, intuitively at least, seem to understand that. There are fewer good jobs left, and people, because of the high number of applicants, apply for them as quickly as possible even before their résumés are fully developed.

Developing a good résumé is difficult for a variety of reasons. Most people are not used to writing about themselves. And they are unsure which aspects of their experiences will be of interest to hiring managers. The first couple of drafts tend to focus on positions held rather than things accomplished. Creating a chronology is easier than detailing the value someone has created over the course of a career. It is easier, in part, because few have learned to focus on value creation. The bureaucracies many work in tend to obscure rather than highlight individual value creation because products are completed in incremental steps by different people at different points in the process. Bureaucracies make it difficult to tell exactly who is responsible for creating the final product and, consequently, difficult to tell who contributed and who did not.

Perhaps you have heard of the Procter & Gamble problem in which no one could explain the unacceptably low level of quality of one of their products. Each of the several departments passing the product along its way to completion reported a 98 percent error-free completion rate. Each was able to argue "not us." The answer was that a 2 percent suboptimization at each stage in a multistage process led to a final product of unacceptable quality. A 2 percent suboptimization in a two-stage process leads to a 96 percent success rate (two to the second power). But the same 2 percent error rate in each stage of a five-stage process (two to the fifth power) leads to a 64 percent success rate.

Bureaucracies work the same way because one of their functions is to divide tasks into their simplest units so as to minimize mistakes. Bureaucratic organizations control risks this way. Many of the corporate bureaucracies developed after World War II mimicked the organizational structures used by the military. These were bureaucracies in which titles were indicators of those being trusted to perform certain control functions, but not necessarily of value creation beyond that. Today companies have figured out that bureaucracies can be both inefficient and expensive, and are moving toward self-directed teams in which workers are needed as much for their people skills as for their technical expertise. In self-directed teams, the ability to influence without authority is an important skill and should be featured on most résumés. An emphasis on command and control is often less appropriate than a focus on teamwork and value creation. Knowing which aspects of one's prior experience to emphasize has become more important than ever. Beyond this, getting a résumé before a pair of human eyes is no easy task. Getting it "read" may only mean it is scanned for key words by a software program. Résumés containing the key words may be passed forward for additional review. Those that do not are discarded. Therefore it is important to know what the key words are. Sometimes key words are related to functional requirements. For example, an employer may program its software to screen for applicants who have "designed and implemented executive compensation programs." Résumés that include "design" without "implementation" or "compensation" without "executive" may be screened out.

Even when résumés get past scanning software, they must overcome other hurdles to get in front of hiring managers. A résumé is like an advertisement in that it is intended to create an initial positive impression inviting the reader to further exploration—perhaps in the form of an interview. If the position has been advertised, there will likely be hundreds of other résumés competing for the same attention. Advertisers know their ads are in competition with others and spend weeks and months getting them right. Résumés, the argument goes, deserve no less attention.

The need for a well-thought-out résumé is increased, not diminished, by technology. In one sense it is far easier today for organizations to connect with applicants for employment and vice versa. Theoretically, it is possible to apply for a position anywhere in the world, making competition for jobs global in scope. Of course, there are limitations to a fully functional global talent pool. While distance is dying, it is not completely dead, and proximity to work is still a consideration. But many of the limitations imposed by proximity may prove to be temporary as they are less limiting than at any time before in human history.

Mary saw herself as being in the advice business, with far too many clients not taking her advice. That is, they were not waiting until their résumés were completely polished to begin applying for jobs. It was further evidence that she needed to rethink her approach.

Yet, there are valid reasons why people are encouraged to take time between sessions to work on their résumés and avoid premature entry into the job market. Mary has given this advice hundreds of times, and hundreds of times it had been ignored. Ready or not, her clients applied for jobs as quickly as they heard about them. Far too many times they sent in poorly written résumés that not only damaged their chances in the application process but also damaged the reputation of the transition counselor as well.

How can the impatience of clients be accounted for? Much of it has to do with heightened levels of anxiety and self-doubt that come with the lack of a steady job, coupled with the need for a sustainable source of income. It may also result from the embarrassment of unemployment. Applying for multiple jobs as quickly as possible improves one's chances of landing at least one of them. There is enough logic behind these assumptions to make starting a broad search as quickly as possible worth a try. The other side of that logic, however, means being exposed as well to more rejection.

At this stage in the process, maintaining a positive attitude gets put ahead of being prepared. That is understandable. Both anxiety and self-doubt are corralled by the quick-landing syndrome—the tendency of people to try and land another job right away rather than take time to do career planning or produce a polished résumé. Being let go is a personal affront that tends to invalidate what people think about themselves. During these times it is convenient to believe that the wrong person was fired, and the best way to prove it is to land another job right away. These feelings are accentuated by sympathetic friends and coworkers anxious to lend emotional support. Helping a fallen comrade by encouraging them to apply for a position that just happened to come up yesterday is a more attractive alternative than polishing one's résumé or contemplating the passion or skills one has for their current career choice.

This is a time when the job search process produces courtesy interviews in quick succession. People want to help, and the interviews serve the function of keeping one's spirits high without necessarily advancing one's immediate job prospects. People enlist the aid of others by asking for courtesy interviews—that is, the opportunity to speak with others to provide more contacts and not necessarily to be referred for jobs. Having been there before, most people are both polite and sympathetic. But there is also the odd chance they may know of an opening for a great job for which one is the perfect candidate. How useful these courtesy interviews end up being usually depends on two variables: who the interviewer is and one's readiness to take advantage.

If the interviewer is one of the connectors Malcolm Gladwell (*The Tipping Point*) discusses,[1] this person can be a valuable resource in a job search. Career counselors advise their clients to have a well-written résumé and a clear career direction before going on courtesy interviews. Anything short of this level of preparation risks an inefficient use of an opportunity and putting a poorly prepared résumé in circulation.

Mary has given up asking her clients to wait until she thinks they are ready and instead has moved the session on résumés forward in the group's transition process. She has taken the additional step of getting out of the "résumé-writing" business altogether. She now directs her clients to the Internet, where they can use any one of several search engines to cover the mechanics of résumé writing. She tells them to use any of several search engines (Google is usually a good choice) and search on the words "résumé writing." That brings up more information than any one individual can ever use. They will find instructions on writing résumés with every slant imaginable, and even services that will write the résumé for them. She directs them to some of the better websites and books (see the Resources section). Her role in that process has been reduced to reviewing each client's résumé as many times as they want. She now spends her time on more value-added discussions with the group.

THE RÉSUMÉ PARADOX

Because the numbers of good jobs have been reduced, with more people chasing them than ever before, the stakes have risen. How résumés actually get used and the ethical questions that inevitably come when important outcomes are uncertain are the issues commanding more of Mary's attention. Bob Watson's elevator speech has given her an excellent bridge for the discussion.

Though still early in the job search process, members of the group are beginning to sense there is a major paradox involved in producing a usable résumé. Writing a good one is hard work. And there is general agreement that a good résumé is an important component of a job search. In reality, a well-written résumé almost never can land a good job, but when written poorly it can cause a candidate to lose a job opportunity. Understanding this paradox is one of the keys to conducting an effective job search. It requires understanding how résumés get weeded out and selected in.

Typically, a job posting attracts more résumés than hiring managers have time to read. They cede that responsibility mostly to staffing professionals who are responsible for putting together slates of candidates who will be interviewed by the hiring manager. Staffing professionals are judged on their ability to put together high-quality candidate slates. As a result, they become the ultimate gatekeepers, letting through only those résumés that hiring managers will view as being worthy. They want to select only those candidates who would be seen as legitimate contenders by the hiring manager. The process encourages a conservative, non-risk-taking approach to hiring that has two sides—weeding out and selecting in. The former is the easier of the two and involves a dirty little secret in the staffing business. Most résumés go the route Jeffrey Fox suggested when he wrote:

> A résumé with a 'for everyman' cover letter is junk mail. A résumé without a cover letter is used to line the bottom of the birdcage. Most direct mail hits the trash barrel between the mailbox and the house. All unexpected and standard résumés go from the in box to the trash box. Some may generate a rejection form letter; most get ignored. 99.2 percent get tossed...[2]

By one estimate, staffing professionals spend on average thirty seconds reviewing a résumé before deciding whether it is worth a second look. Actually, most résumés do not get read at all. In the normal course of things, the chance that any one résumé will stand out in the pile is remote.

People ask, why then spend so much time producing a prime-time document when hiring managers do not even read them? The answer is in understanding how résumés get selected in. A final slate has no more than six candidates. Six may even be seen as too burdensome for some organizations. But six is not a large number when viewed against an initial applicant pool of a hundred or more—and a hundred is a conservative estimate for an online application process. Staffing professionals are instructed to put slates together with candidates who already have experience doing what the hiring manager wants and proof of having done it well. Seasoned staffing professionals will ask the hiring manager to put forward any candidates she may have in mind. This encourages ownership of the slate beyond the staffing department—an important consideration if filling the position takes longer than expected. Of course, it always does, but taking longer is okay when one or two are candidates suggested by the hiring manager herself.

Those high-quality networking referrals discussed earlier also come into play. Those who happen to have the right credentials and have been referred into the hiring process from a valued and trusted source have dramatically improved chances of having their résumés read in earnest. Some may see this as confirmation of the old adage, "It is not what you know, but who you know that counts." This is not so. It is just that good referrals are more reliable than good résumés for producing qualified candidates. Consequently, personal referrals are components of any reasonably acceptable slate of candidates.

The other dynamic of slate-building revolves around the inclusion of minorities and women. Hiring managers and staffing professionals are expected to have candidate slates that are inclusive. At the end of the year or any particular hiring process, they will likely be asked, "Did you include any minority or female applicants?" This aspect of the process feels like reverse discrimination to some. A more accurate view is that it is an expression of the process of withdrawing permission from the organization to exclude these groups as they may have in the past. Women and minorities were once excluded with impunity. To now insist upon their inclusion feels like favoritism, when actually they are being culled out from the ravages of past practices.

Those surviving the weeding out and selecting in processes now only hope they have a résumé that will stand the test of further scrutiny. To have gotten in as a referral only to submit a résumé full of typos, or one that focuses on command-and-control skills at the expense of the team, can put a candidate in a weak position relative to others. As noted above, a good résumé will not necessarily get someone onto a candidate slate, but a poorly written or conceived one can push them off.

RÉSUMÉS AS BRANDING INSTRUMENTS

A well-written résumé is a step toward establishing one's personal brand. A personal brand is what someone is known for—one's reputation. In a world of instantaneous access, brand becomes more, not less, important. Frances Cairncross (*The Death of Distance*) reminded us that technology gives the advantage to consumers, as they have greater access to higher quality goods and services at cheaper prices.[3] Brand becomes even more of an organizing principle by which consumption choices are made. The same applies in reverse. The availability of talent on a global basis gives organizations choices. Application pools in which there are a hundred candidates for a single position gives the advantage to the employer. The personal brands of the applicants become a focal point in the decision-making process. This is another reason why referrals from trusted associates are a preferred method of preparing candidate slates. Since many referrals are from people known and trusted by someone in the hiring process, the people they refer often have better brand identity vis-à-vis those who applied directly without knowing anyone. Their résumés become the initial means by which their reputations are confirmed.

People in transition as well as those just starting out will find the concept useful. But using a résumé as a branding tool sits at the edge of a paradigm shift in our relationship to jobs and careers. As workers have become more expendable, résumés are used to create advantage in the competition for jobs. This is not the advantage that comes with just having experience. Many people will likely have the experience needed to do a particular job. Rather than simple summaries of positions held, résumés now need to be bold statements about value creation.

Some hiring managers accept the idea of résumés as an extension of brand management and some do not. However, for both, the appearance of exaggerated claims will be a red flag. Astute job-seekers (brand managers) must now learn how to brag without appearing to be boastful. The résumé is one of the primary tools available for this purpose. A résumé is a means of extending one's brand to people with whom they have otherwise not been connected. Once used for this purpose, the ethics of résumé writing become more important.

What obligation do companies have to consumers regarding claims they make about their brand? The companion question is, what obligation do those who prepare résumés have to their intended audiences? Tobacco companies advertised smoking as fun and as a way to get a piece of the good life. What obligation do they have to the consuming public? The answers have changed over time. Earlier they were seen as having no public health obligation at all. What about fast-food or soda companies? Does McDonald's have an obligation in its brand management to give advice to children (one of their primary targets) regarding the health risk of eating its products in excess? How those looking for work manage their personal brands will not likely be the subject of litigation or public policy. But some of the issues consumer product companies deal with involve principles that have applications to personal brand management as well.

RÉSUMÉ LIES

The easiest of all advice to give is, do not lie on your résumé. Most people would agree that lying is not an ethical choice. Yet it happens frequently. The most common lie usually has to do with educational credentials one thinks they need in order to qualify for a position but do not have. Since some organizations do not conduct background checks, it is possible to get away with it on occasion. Some people claim to have degrees at all levels up to and including PhD. Once a lie gets told, there is a tendency to keep on telling it. As time goes by, correcting the lie becomes more difficult. Perhaps the saddest of these stories are about people with otherwise distinguished careers, whose credibility and means of livelihood are diminished once they are found out.

At a time in which brand is more important than ever, the damage a lie can inflict on one's reputation is worth considering. Before the last technological iteration, lies were more easily buried as there was no convenient way to check. The Internet has made checking easier, and once a lie is exposed, it has made it almost impossible to hide from others.

Doing business on eBay is a case in point. eBay is as close to a self-governing market as we have today. People stake their reputations on each business transaction because others have a chance to post comments about their experiences. People with good brands have a lot easier time making their fortunes on eBay compared with those who fail to provide quality goods and services.

MANAGING GAPS IN EMPLOYMENT HISTORY

Job-seekers are also concerned about explaining gaps in their employment histories, and employers often prefer applicants who are otherwise gainfully employed. Even when employers do not object, out-of-work applicants will be asked to explain why they are not currently unemployed. The norm is that companies will not object to modest gaps in employment. Some companies do occasionally express a preference for people who are already employed or not in the job market. But it is still possible to get onto those candidate slates when referred through the right channels.

Most of the angst about employment gaps comes from applicants who are trying to become reemployed quickly and who are caught in a self-imposed time warp that views being terminated as a personal statement about individual self-worth. Society as a whole readily accepts that most terminations occur as the result of forces beyond an individual's control. Terminations are easily positioned this way because companies that terminate employees are anxious to cooperate in facilitating their reemployment. Such cooperation helps their reputation in the market.

The way a résumé is written can provide a good opportunity to obscure significant gaps in employment. Is this ethical? Yes, but it is the wrong question. Let us first deal with how it is done, and then pursue the ethics of the matter.

Since it is an accepted practice to write résumés in yearly time increments, most gaps upward of two years do not appear and need not be reported or highlighted. For example, the situations below show two résumé timelines, one including months and one written in years.

EXAMPLE #1
- June 1995–Feb. 1997: Director, Quality Control
- March 1997–November 1997: Unemployed.
- Dec. 1997–Present: Vice President, Quality Assurance.

EXAMPLE #2
- 1995–1997: Director, Quality Control
- 1997–Present: Vice President, Quality Assurance

While we would not expect the gap to be announced as a line item as in Example #1, leaving it out still shows an obvious period of time of unemployment. Both timelines are correct. One example raises the question. The other does not. Most people do not go out of their way to show gaps in employment.

Is it appropriate to mislead by implication? That is, a résumé using yearly time frames gives the impression of continuous employment when there could have been almost two full years of unemployment. Without question, some gap in employment is acceptable. In these times, when employers aggressively manage their profitability through dramatic and sometimes frequent adjustments to their cost of human capital, it is unrealistic to expect truly continuous employment histories. How large a gap to mention is left for each individual to decide. But let us be clear. Using yearly time frames is absolutely fine, but of less importance than we sometimes believe. Someone in transition is, by definition, in the midst of a job gap, some of which can be covered by résumé gymnastics. However, the real question is not whether someone has an employment gap, but rather, what does one do with it. This time can be used in numerous admirable ways that our schedules had not allowed before. These include travel, building family relationships, religious activity, or supporting worthy charities. It is possible to look for work while being engaged in these activities. Explaining gaps in the context of important priorities will, to some employers, show strength of character rather than weakness of skill sets.

Over the years I have spoken with hundreds of clients who have effectively managed their employment gaps by claiming themselves to be "consultants." This leaves the door open for doing occasional consulting in their areas of expertise. The obvious downside to this approach is the tendency of some to substantially reduce the time put into looking for a job. On the other hand, I have known of people whose consulting skills were so substantial, they developed a sustainable consulting practice without really intending to do so.

TOO OLD OR NOT?

People age fifty or older and in transition worry about age discrimination. Should they? Yes, they should. Age discrimination exists and can be a real problem. Some industries (such as IT) are notorious for having a preference for younger workers. Discussion groups and political activists in every industrialized country in the world focus on this issue. Most of them are looking to enact the kind of legislation present in the United States. This is done for good reason. It works.

There is little evidence to support any conclusion of systematic discrimination against people fifty and older as companies in the United States go out of their way to avoid giving the appearance of discrimination. In large measure this is true because of various state and federal laws against it. Companies that actively discriminate fail to take advantage of experienced workers and risk the imposition of hefty penalties to their public image and financial well-being.

The extent to which one should be concerned about losing out on jobs because of age very much depends on the industry, economic conditions, and the experience brought to the marketplace. The more senior the position, the fewer the number of jobs available and the more rejection will feel like age discrimination. For example, recently in California the number of age discrimination complaints rose. Rather than being an indication of more actual age discrimination, according to Margaret Steen, a feature writer for the *San Jose Mercury News,* a number of factors appear to be operating here, including:

- An increase in the number of workers eligible to file claims.
- The numbers of complaints actually declining in one county, in particular.
- A lower unemployment rate for older workers meaning the job market is actually better for older workers.
- The concentration of high-tech industries, a market segment that has a reputation for hiring younger workers and letting older ones go.
- Survey results by the AARP that showed most companies treated the résumés of older and younger applicants essentially the same, though a substantial minority preferred younger workers.[4]

There is also evidence to suggest that discrimination is less prevalent when demand for labor is perceived to exceed the supply. Perceived resistance in the marketplace does not automatically mean that one's fears about being too old are grounded in reality. In fact, between 1999 and 2002, the Equal

Employment Opportunity Commission (EEOC), the national agency responsible for enforcement of the Age Discrimination in Employment Act of 1967, found only 17 percent of complaints coming to them had merit. There are positions available to older workers, and we have every reason to believe that most employers understand and abide by the law. Since discrimination on the basis of age is illegal and fewer companies do it than believed, having an age-neutral résumé is not as critical as many believe. Those who want to hedge their bets should feel free to adjust their résumés accordingly. This can be done by eliminating unnecessary references to dates of education, certifications, and other activities. Any work experiences beyond twelve years can be summarized and presented as a collection of experiences that enhance one's current skill set. My sense is that most companies are not really interested in, for example, when you got your degree so much as what value you will bring to their organization and how long you will be an effective worker. To this extent age can be a factor. Your appearance and demeanor will likely be more important than age. But keep in mind; you are who you are. Be proud of that and present yourself to the marketplace as someone who is of value and worth considering for employment. Whether you are 25 or 65, or more, companies will at some time know how old you are.

Questions about having had too many jobs or too few are different sides of the same coin. What was looked upon a few years ago as job-hopping is now viewed more positively as adaptability and a willingness to work in different environments. It is more acceptable today to have changed jobs several times. Companies merge, outsource, and downsize more often. Staffing professionals are more understanding and accepting of others who change jobs because there is a good possibility it has happened to them. So, multiple jobs within a relatively short period do not automatically arouse suspicion. As with anything, changing jobs can be overdone. If that happens, reasonable explanations are expected.

People in the job market with twenty or more years with a single employer have another set of challenges. Not only is there no gold watch, but there is also the suspicion that their skills are stale. Those who sense this should emphasize the different positions and accomplishments they have experienced over the course of their company tenure. They need to demonstrate a rich diversity of experiences over many years of good service.

THE CREATIVE RÉSUMÉ

Sometimes résumés are submitted with the intention of being separate and distinct from others in the stack. These are usually creative résumés and come in endless variations too numerous to detail. Is the submission of a creative résumé an effective means of making the cut? There are positions in the creative arts and certain areas of design, music, and perhaps public relations for which a creative résumé is a demonstration of the ability to perform. How creative one wants to be is up to the individual. It is best to think of it from the perspective of the interviewer; does receiving a creative résumé give someone an excuse to weed it out or select it in? To the extent that such résumés are truly unusual, exclusion will win in a large percentage of the cases.

Again, the use of creative résumés begs the wrong question. When used as a leave-behind document, the question of the appropriate degree of creativity should have already been answered. That is, during the process of being selected in, one should have gotten the lay of the land and a sense of how a creatively constructed résumé would be received. Just as with more standard résumés, a well-written one will not likely land a job, but a poorly written one can lose it. There is a good chance that an unexpected creative résumé will be viewed as little more than being in poor taste.

Can résumés be used to make the case for changing careers? The correct answer is probably not. Such a change is, at best, difficult. Some experts argue that résumés need to be forward-looking documents focusing on what someone wants to do and not on what they have done. A functional résumé is suggested in these instances. Most people, however, read résumés with the expectation of finding a strong linkage between the position they are trying to fill and previous positions the candidate has had. While a desire to change careers may be of paramount importance to the applicant, it is not likely to be important to the hiring manager. If they are looking for cross-functional experience (as many employers are), it will show up in a more traditional résumé. The greater the gap between past experience and new career direction, the more difficult it is to use a résumé as a tool to establish a viable candidacy or rebrand oneself. This reinforces the more general notion of using a résumé as a leave-behind document rather than as a method of introduction.

Functional résumés are neither the norm nor are they preferred in most cases. They are viewed most often as attempts to camouflage and thus arouse suspicion rather than create trust and interest. This view is mostly correct because a functional grouping of experiences is a way of directing the attention of the reader away one's job chronology toward other more salient aspects of the work experience. But all résumés are directive in this respect. It is just that one format is acceptable and one invites suspicion.

THE EMBELLISHED RÉSUMÉ

How far to go in embellishing one's accomplishments is another issue people confront. It is easy to understand how lying is both unethical and a high-risk game most choose not to play. Embellishments present a different set of issues. Often there is a thin line between an embellishment and an outright lie. How might one stay on the appropriate side of that line?

Claiming credit for the accomplishments of others is clearly inappropriate. In many organizations it is often difficult to tell who is responsible for what and who has earned the right to take credit. Is being in charge synonymous with being responsible for the value created in a particular organization? We have all heard of places that accomplish their objectives in spite of their leadership, not because of it. There are virtually no guidelines for determining what to take credit for. Here is a thought. We work in environments in which teamwork is required and expected. When we take credit for things accomplished, it makes reasonable sense to recognize the roles others played as well. Second, a good way to avoid runaway embellishments is to ask: How might those I worked with respond to the claims on my résumé? Would they agree? Am I prepared to have the discussion with them about the role I played and the resulting value created? How would the potential for having that discussion change what I claim? Whether one has the conversations or not, asking the question and working through the answers will help keep one on the right side of the embellishment line.

Sending out résumés en masse is also not an effective job-hunting device. Rather, résumés are leave-behind documents that reinforce a more personal set of contacts. The how-to literature and job search professionals have covered this point fairly well. In fact, the entire résumé-writing process has now lapsed into the category of being a commodity service available online. However, the transition profession has yet to catch up with some of the ethical issues that are raised, as those in transition are required to use their résumés as personal branding instruments. How anyone chooses to construct theirs is a matter of personal ethics.

CHAPTER SEVEN

୶

NETWORKING, INTERVIEWING,
AND NEGOTIATING

MARY'S GROUP, WITH résumés in hand, move forward with their job searches as if matching wits against some invisible hand. At least it feels that way sometimes. It would be easier if the invisible hand would just match résumés against open positions. In some respects, that is exactly what is happening when the Internet is used to conduct a job search. The problem is that it does not work very well. The Internet is an amazing creation full of potential uses that are yet to be perfected. Using it to find a job is one of those. With a search engine, such as Google, and a high-speed Internet line, one can find a remarkable selection of job openings. For example, "job search" yields over a million references in just .12 seconds. The site for Career Builder has an advertisement for 1.3 million jobs available online, with "new jobs added daily." The Australian government has a website listing jobs by territory. There are over 27,000 jobs in New South Wales and another 1,200 in Tasmania. One can find cool jobs in Canada and hot jobs in Hong Kong. There are jobs in engineering, accounting, and education—jobs in companies that are pro-gay and pro-Christian. If someone did not know better, they would think it is possible to scrap the entire search process, save for résumé writing, and do the entire search online. However, comparatively few jobs are gotten by using the Internet. People who spend most of their job search time surfing the net are looked at as having given up on finding a job.

The process by which résumés bubble to the top is not changed by the Internet, it is reinforced by it. Staffing professionals still must put together candidate slates with usually no more than six candidates. Having access to more résumés because of the Internet only increases the difficulty applicants have in getting their résumés noticed and to the top of the stack.

Once the résumé has been completed, the basic steps involved in a job search are the same now as they were twenty years ago; connecting to the job market in a way that gets one's candidacy noticed, interviewing, and negotiating the terms of employment. However, the process is not as linear as it appears. That is, job-seekers may revisit each step again and again as they move through the process. For example, once people truly understand the concept of value creation, they frequently want to draft another résumé and reconnect with potential employers to clarify previous discussions.

NETWORKING

Connecting with people for purposes of career management is known in the industry as networking and is the sacred cow of the career transition business. Its virtues are universally acclaimed, and people sometimes are encouraged to travel thousands of miles to attend networking meetings. However, a less flattering perspective on this method of looking for work is beginning to emerge.

Networking consists of a set of awkward activities most of us will never master or get comfortable using. In a more limited sense, it works, but it is not a tool most of us can use with enough skill and dexterity to justify its position as the cornerstone of the career counseling profession. There are other ways of getting the results of networking that do not require a full deployment of its techniques. At its best, networking is a tool of limited utility. At its worst, it is a way for people in transition to keep their spirits up by staying busy. To understand why, let us take a look at what traditional networking promises its users as compared with what people actually experience. We will then discuss some second thoughts about the process in the new economy.

The lead-in to the subject of networking on the website for QuintCareers.com is indicative of what career transition professionals believe about networking and the results they expect to get.

> Networking is one of the most important—if not the most important—activities that job-seekers need to master to be truly successful in your job search. Because the vast majority of job openings are never advertised, job-seekers need to have a network of contacts—a career network—that can provide support, information and job leads.[1]

The value of networking is supported by oft-quoted statistics. All three major career transition firms—Drake Beam Morin (DBM), Right Management Consultants (RMC), and Lee Hecht Harrison (LHH)—report that anywhere from 64 to 80 percent of jobs people in transition report getting come from people they know, that is, from networking. Networking is seen as being so powerful that job-seekers are advised to keep their networks alive once re-employed. Michelle Tullier in her how-to guide *Networking for Job Search and Career Success* defines what networking is and is not. According to her:

> It is not about being pushy, and it is not a contest to see who can collect the most business cards or shake the most hands. It is not a one-sided, selfish, flash-in-the-pan activity.... True networking—effective networking—is based on relationships

that are cultivated and nurtured so that a mutual exchange of information, advice, referrals and support takes place.[2]

Networking has also been described as an activity one does for future benefit. That is, people are advised to network and establish relationships before they need them in a job search situation. This view is supported by Richard Bolles (*Parachute*) who advised, "[the purpose of networking is to] . . . gather a list of contacts now that might be able to help you with your career or with your job hunting, at some future date."[3] The logic of networking is compelling, and career transition professionals advocate its use across the board by everyone. We are told that refusing to network will evidently cause us to miss out on the hidden job market. This is serious given that the hidden job market reputedly is where most of the white-collar jobs reside. They are hidden because they are seldom advertised. While it is difficult to tell just how much of the job market is really hidden, taking the chance on missing it by not networking may be too much of a risk. So network we will, if network we must. Or, must we? What we know of networking includes that it: provides access to the hidden job market and is where most of the white-collar jobs are; is important to establish meaningful (strong) professional relationships of mutual respect and exchange; and, is an activity that will make future job searches easier.

I remember giving a presentation a few years ago on the virtues of networking to a group of supply-chain specialists in Chicago. Afterward, one brave soul was kind enough to let me know there were likely two kinds of people in the audience; half who did not know what networking was, and the other half who knew, but did not have the slightest idea of how to go about doing it. This experience was brought to mind in Barbara Ehrenreich's book, *Bait and Switch*. She reports finding it all but impossible to get more than one or two contacts at a networking meeting in spite of the meetings being specifically advertised for that purpose. She suggested that networking did not take place in the meetings she attended for either of two reasons. Either they were poorly designed (i.e., no time left for networking after the personal testimonials), or there was another agenda (religious proselytizing).[4] I agree and offer an additional explanation: Networking, for the vast majority of people, is an uncomfortable experience. Some of you will smile when you read this, because you know how difficult it is for you. Others may disagree. Consider this: My observation is that there are very few among us who can effectively network an entire room. This is true if the room is filled with family members or complete strangers. Furthermore, those who network aggressively within the family tend to be the same ones who do so in a room of strangers. From this perspective, good networkers do not need encouragement to network. They do it naturally. However, very *few* of us are really good networkers.

Once reemployed, people report that networking is the first thing they stop doing, in spite of advice to the contrary. Even when others are being laid off around them, people will only reluctantly, if at all, return to networking. Those who have gone through outplacement before and who have not maintained their networks develop a sense of guilt. Refusing to remain an active networker is a little like refusing to stay in the habit of regular exercise. Networking is something most of us cannot do well and stop doing the minute we can.

The way the numbers on networking are reported, we do not learn much about the process, only the purported results. Fortunately, Tiller's book gives us some clues about the process. She writes: "Networking is not about superficial connections and brief encounters. It is about cultivating relationships with others in a meaningful way so that you have people to turn to when you need information and support and people you can help when they need someone to turn to."[5]

What could possibly be wrong with that? It is imbued with our religious and moral ethic. In fact, suggesting that it may not be true almost seems counterintuitive.

The conventional wisdom put forth by networking advocates tells people to network when they are in transition and to keep networking even after they find employment. As a person networks, they should be looking for more than superficial connections and brief encounters. The advice invariably ends up being ignored by everyone except those who do not need the advice in the first place. In this context, networking becomes an unwanted source of guilt.

Tuller and others advise us to make our networking ties meaningful. By this they seem to mean that strong ties are preferable to weak ones. This might not be true. Malcolm Gladwell in *The Tipping Point* made the observation that a majority (55.6%) of those who found a job through personal connections did so through weak ties. That is, they got jobs through having ties with acquaintances they saw only occasionally.[6] Two points jump out: Getting a job through personal contacts works, and ties to those contacts do not have to be particularly strong. Networking may not work the way it has been implied. It may be that we do not have to be fully adept at establishing meaningful relationships in order to find jobs through people.

The research Gladwell cites by sociologist Mark Granovetter (*The Strength of Weak Ties*) has been available since 1974, but has largely gone unused (unread?) by the career transition industry. Whom one connects with may be more important than the strength of the connection. These are people Gladwell refers to as connectors. Perhaps you have met some of them without knowing it. They are the people who, once you have told them, you might as well have told everybody. Some of them are busybodies, but most are not. They are people who seem to know everybody and are valued for their knowledge. They tend to be connected to large networks of people at various levels throughout the socioeconomic spectrum, and who are respected for being high-quality channels of information. Connectors are people who have the capability to spread things far and wide and, what better people to know you want a job than they.

Job search consultants (headhunters) tend to be natural connectors. They seem to know everybody and often refer people to jobs even though there is no fee. They know the jobs that are open and the people who can fill them. And if they do not happen to be familiar with exactly the right person, they can find them. The currency they trade in is high-quality information gotten from a wide variety of sources, especially from people with whom they have weak ties. The pecking order in the search business usually values retained search (firms that are retained and paid, even if no one is hired) over those doing contingency work (firms that are paid only if the person they referred is hired). While it is true that the former usually deal with higher levels of jobs and get higher fees, it is not true that they are better connectors than their contingency brethren.

Not all connectors are in the search business. In fact, most of them are not. Sometimes they are accountants, engineers, lawyers, human resource professionals, clergy, barbers, politicians, bridge players, carpenters, civil servants, stay-at-home moms, or just plain folks who connect with a lot of other people. They have high-quality information and a broad network in common. People call them to get information and to get their word out. John Lucht (*The Rites of Passage*) reminds us of what a connector does and how she operates when in the introduction to his book he devotes an entire page to one sentence saying, "This is what I tell my friends."[7] What follows is a book full of inside information on how to change jobs. The information is not reserved for a select few, nor is it different from the information he would provide his very best friends. It is the quality of the information and not the strength of the relationship that determines its usefulness. Lucht, like other connectors, is a conduit for information. He is valued for its quality. Furthermore, the information he makes available to his friends he also makes available to those with whom he has weaker ties, the readers of his book.

One implication for networking (connecting) is that whom one connects with is critically important. Rather than connecting with everyone or even just with others in the same profession, it is more useful to connect with connectors. The main feature of connecting is that it is also easier to do. Connectors are often as interested in meeting you and as you are in meeting them. You will recognize them because in conversations you have with co-workers and friends their names would have come up more than other names. While you have to do a little work to find out who they are, it is easier than landing a courtesy interview with just anybody. In fact, use those courtesy interviews to find the connectors and where they hang out. Will they attend the next meeting of auditing professionals? Are they members of the softball league? Get the point?

Connecting with connectors is networking in a sense. But it is networking in which the burden of establishing meaningful relationships is shifted to being content with weaker ties that are easier to establish and maintain. At the next meeting of your professional association, the connectors should be easy to spot. They are the ones working the room and who will get around to you eventually. In most instances, all you have to do is stand next to them. If you do nothing else, be sure you meet the connectors.

Before connecting, it is helpful to understand something of the value one creates and how to bring that value to the attention of others. This is not easy and is probably one of the most difficult things job-seekers will have to do. The requirement-of-context is a part of what makes this difficult and where the idea of one's personal brand comes most prominently into play.

Take Miesha Collins (not her real name). She is the receptionist in an office in the Right Management Consulting system. The best description I ever heard of her came from one of our clients, who described her as the tie-breaker. At Right, we went out of our way to attract high-end executives in transition. The business is very profitable and often leads to additional op-portunities once they are reemployed. They usually visit (shop) three or four transition firms several times to decide which one is the best fit for them. But our clients tell us that all the outplacement firms look and sound alike. They make the same claims and use the same job search methodologies. Once someone decided to work with Right, we always asked, why? The hope was, we would find a common theme we could then take to market more con-sistently and land even greater numbers of these prized clients. A surprising number of shoppers choosing Right mentioned Miesha's warm and friendly personality. Once she got to know them, she remembered their names as well as those of their spouses and children. She genuinely cared about them and always had a can-do attitude when something needed to get done.

Miesha's reputation (personal brand) is not as a receptionist, but as a tie-breaker. It is a brand that easily translates into value, and when referred to a connector becomes a form of currency for the connector because they know someone who is among the best in the business. The conversation a connector might have with someone from a company in need of a receptionist, or any other public-facing job, is not difficult to imagine. "We are really struggling with filling our job at the front desk. Do you know of any good candidates?"

"Let me tell you about my friend, the tiebreaker."

The difficulty Miesha might have is finding a way to talk about the value she creates and getting that across in an interview. Notice, I did not say getting that across in a résumé. Résumés are not a particularly good medium for establishing value.

I would add to Bolles's advice that people should figure out what they are good at. They should also clarify the value they create for others and practice talking about it. People who can create value and establish that as a key component of their personal brand will stay in demand longer and be less subject to the vagaries of outsourcing and downsizing. Their résumés have a better chance of finding their way to the top of the stack.

Should one focus on networking or connecting? They can do either, but chances are they will do only one. If networking is the process of developing and maintaining strong ties to be used later in a job search, there is a good chance that people will not be able to sustain the level of activity necessary to establish strong ties. Strong ties work when trying to find employment. But weak ones work just as well and perhaps even better. When looking for a job, find out where the open positions are by accessing the so-called hidden job market, reading newspaper ads and online postings, or talking to a connector. In all instances, there will likely be a stack of résumés for hiring managers to review. It is just that in the hidden market the stack is smaller, and it easier to get a résumé at or near the top. One's chances of being noticed are better. Having a well-done résumé at this point is imperative.

Natural networkers already live an existence of ongoing connectivity. For the rest—a clear majority and then some—it is helpful to do the little things day in and day out that are short of a full-fledged effort, but keeps them in their comfort zone enough to avoid the traditional pitfalls of networking. This advice is relevant for people in transition, those gainfully employed, and others just starting careers. The latter group is often an afterthought for career transition professionals. They are impacted as well, as we begin to feel the effects of globalization on long-term employment prospects for new entrants into the job market.

People at all points along the career continuum will find it useful to incorporate sound career management practices into their everyday lives. Nonstop networking is out of the question. As such, a more natural way to get the advantages of constructive career management is for people to STRETCH to their futures by committing to any one of a number of less intrusive activities. This entails doing a check-in on a monthly or weekly basis on the following activities:

Stay current with your profession or industry to make sure you understand the issues of the day. This may mean reading an article or two once a month from a professional journal or newspaper articles about current trends. It is not necessary that you do anything with this information immediately. But you will soon be surprised at your ability to anticipate what will happen and begin preparing for it.

Take your personal brand seriously. Take a look at that last performance evaluation and reread it with an eye toward whether it formally recognizes you for contributions that are of fundamental importance to the mission of the organization. Remember, Miesha Collins is known for being a "tiebreaker"—a personal brand directly related to the mission of the organization and one that easily translates into value for other organizations.

Reach out to the connectors of the world. Get to know as many as you can because they are the ones others rely on for information and referrals.

Expand your brand. That is, expand what you are known for as well as by whom. If possible, make sure you are known by a broader spectrum of people than you currently are connected with.

Talk about the value you create. Find out who the people are in the organization in which you work (as well as other organizations you are associated with) that are respected and valued for the contributions they make to achieving organizational goals. Ask yourself what you would have to do in your position to get a similar response from people about your contribution.

Create value. Once you understand value creation, you can do it.

Have it your way. If you are like most of us, you can not/will not do all of the things suggested here all of the time. Do the one, two, or three things as often as you can just to get started. Remember, doing one is better than doing none. Start with what you feel most comfortable with.

These things are simple, but not simple-minded. We are in the midst of one of the most significant transitions in the history of the world in which the competitive playing field is being leveled. What each of us must do to make a living and manage our careers is changing.

INTERVIEWING

Once someone has developed an effective résumé and connected with job opportunities, the next step is to prepare for job interviews. Effective interviewing is a tricky business, largely because feedback is given only when the interview goes well. Why? Because staffing professionals are too smart to go into any detail with people about why they have been rejected. This is for good reason. They do not have the time to engage and educate each and every candidate about their interviewing skills. Besides, there is no percentage in telling people they failed. Instead, the safest route is to acknowledge that the interview went well and that "while your credentials were impressive, we found other candidates whose backgrounds and experiences more closely fit our requirements." In other words the interviewee did not fail; there just were better-qualified applicants. Sometimes organizations make the mistake of telling people that they are overqualified. Any feedback to the negative will at best incite disagreement and anger. At worst the company may be subject to claims of having used inappropriate criteria for job selection. Candor does not pay.

The inability to get accurate feedback from interviews accounts for the substantial amount of help available from the how-to literature. Most of the books and articles cover the same material and are directed toward a broad audience. At the most elementary levels people are told to be on time, dress neatly, and be observant. In fact, there seems to be a little of this advice in the literature at all levels.

One level up from that has advice about how to answer questions. Why should I hire you? What are your career goals? What qualities should good managers have? What do you know about us? What is the biggest mistake you ever made? The list is too long; and getting ready for more than a few will more likely confuse rather than clarify. In the end, people are advised to just be aware of the general categories of questions so if one hears them in an interview it will not be for the first time.

The very best of the interviewing literature advises its readers to prepare by doing research on the organization as well as the individuals they are scheduled to see. They should know why the position is open and how their background and experience fit. They should know what the organization is trying to accomplish by filling the position and resist any discussion of salary because being either too high or too low is used by some companies to weed out applicants. If companies insist on knowing salary history as a precondition for being considered, people are advised to provide the appropriate information without hesitation.

As a whole, the interviewing literature has made a substantial contribution to the career transition body of knowledge. In an earlier time, white-collar workers in particular did not have to be particularly skilled in either writing résumés or interviewing. As people began changing jobs, they needed to be more skillful about these things, and the career transition/career management industry provided that information. Again, it is not that the literature missed its mark; it is that the mark has changed.

Increasing competition for jobs has redefined the job market of today as being about brand. On the employee side of the ledger, it is about one's personal reputation; about the ability to create value as well as the ability to talk about the value one creates.

Miesha might have the following response to the question: Why should we hire you?

"I see myself as a receptionist, but people tell me I do more than that. They tell me I am a 'tiebreaker.' That is, when high-margin/high-value clients are looking for a reason to choose one firm over another, they tell me I break the tie. Any place I work or volunteer, I try and understand the mission of the organization and how what I do contributes to that. Sometimes I contribute by giving a friendly smile to whoever shows up at the front desk. At other times I do it by showing a sense of urgency on client projects even though they tell me it is not a rush job.

My job is to help. If that is what you need, and it is important, that could be the reason you should hire me. From what I have seen, this is an exciting organization I would like to contribute to."

Is it really realistic to expect an answer like that from an applicant for a receptionist position? Sure it is, especially with a little practice in talking about value creation. The answer would fit a wide variety of circumstances and situations. In today's flatter organizations, everyone from the receptionist to the CEO needs to be clear about the value they create and learn to talk about that value to others.

On the employer side, the situation is slightly different. In a typical job-filling process, there are multiple applicants for any one opening. They all are likely to make the same claims about being a good fit for the organization and having the experience to do just that. Getting the stack of applicants down to a manageable few is what the process is about when viewed from the perspective of the employer. Some candidates will be referred by trusted friends. One or two will have worked for known competitors in similar jobs. Others may have just caught the eye of the staffing manager. Regardless, the process is one of differentiating one candidate from another. In the final analysis, it will come down to the one candidate who differentiates herself enough to be the clear choice.

The ability to differentiate among people is something large, successful organizations especially understand. Even if they do not do it well, they understand its importance. It was the subject of differentiation that prompted Jack Welch to say:

> When managers put their necks on the line for their direct reports, you learn as much about them as the people you are discussing. Sometimes we can debate for an hour over one page. Why are these sessions so intense? One word, differentiation. In manufacturing, we try and stamp out variance. With people, variance is everything.[8]

People at GE, according to Welch, are differentiated on four variables: energy levels; the ability to energize others; the edge to make tough decisions; and the ability to execute. The hiring process in well-run organizations is no less important and no less intense. The ability to differentiate one applicant from another and accurately predict who will create value is a critically important function on which careers are built.

In this context, interviewing is more than being on time, wearing the proper attire, or even doing solid research on the organization. It is the one critical time you as the interviewee have to differentiate yourself from others—and vice versa. It is a chance to present your brand and the value you have created.

The concept of differentiation is not well established in the career counseling business. Consequently we must look elsewhere for guiding principles and see if we can bend them to our use. Jack Trout's book *Differentiate or Die: Survival in Our Era of Killer Competition*,[9] with a little modification, goes a long way toward filling the void. His discussion dovetails perfectly with much of the literature on globalization. He essentially agrees that consumers are the winners in the outcome of globalization and the revolution in technology. The consumer has more price-competitive choices than ever before. Trout refers to this as the "Tyranny of Choices" as he chronicles an explosion of choice between the early 1970s and the late 1990s.

For companies needing to differentiate themselves from the competition, Trout advises: "The customer has so many good alternatives and . . . companies pay dearly for their mistakes." Guess what? When there are between 100 to 500 applicants for a single job, the explosion of choice goes to the other side, and the failure of the applicant to differentiate may cause him to pay dearly.

Let us take a look at some of the principles detailed in Trout's book and see what the implications are for people in the midst of looking for work or

Table 7.1 The Explosion of Choice

Item	Early 1970s	Late 1990s
Vehicle models	140	260
KFC menus items	7	14
Frito-Lay chip varieties	10	78
PC models	0	400
Soft drink brands	20	87
Websites	0	4.8M
Bottled water brands	16	50
Airports	11,261	18,202
New book titles	40,530	77,446
Amusement parks	362	1,174
TV screen sizes	5	185
Running shoe styles	5	90
McDonald's items	13	43

Excerpted from Jack Trout, *Differentiate or Die: Survival in our Era of Killer Competition*. New York: John Wiley & Sons; 2000, p. 6.

managing a career. Six principles on branding stand out as having particular applicability. Each is stated (A) and then rephrased (B) in career management language.

A. QUALITY IS A GIVEN, NOT A DIFFERENCE
B. COMPETENCE IS A GIVEN, NOT A DIFFERENCE

It is reasonable to assume that there is an abundance of people available who have the technical competence to do any job for which one might apply. People cannot expect, therefore, to be differentiated on the basis of their technical skill set. There was a time when people might have gained an advantage based on the school attended, mentoring relationships, and prior employment. Those times are fading. The leveling of the playing field continues to reduce those factors in favor of reputation (brand) and value creation. Interviewing on the strength of one's formal credentials will no longer, in most instances, be sufficient to provide differentiation.

A. DIFFERENTIATION IS NOT KNOWING ABOUT YOUR CUSTOMER. IT IS YOUR CUSTOMER KNOWING ABOUT YOU.
B. DIFFERENTIATION IS NOT KNOWING ABOUT THE ORGANIZATION. IT IS THE ORGANIZATION KNOWING ABOUT YOU.

It is easier for an applicant to differentiate herself if the organization knows her through a trusted source or otherwise by reputation. Think about your reputation and how well you might be known in the organization to which you are applying. If you are relatively unknown compared with other applicants, your chances are diminished. Under such circumstances, it is helpful to have a well-established reputation that catches the eye of someone in the organization. Your interviewing strategy should include a way to get your brand better known. If not, at least be able to talk fluently about your reputation in way that piques the collective curiosity of the organization. Being a "tiebreaker" might just do the trick.

A. TODAY, THERE ARE TOO MANY PRODUCTS CHASING TOO FEW CUSTOMERS
B. TODAY, THERE ARE TOO MANY PEOPLE CHASING TOO FEW JOBS

Cutting through the crowd often requires having a unique selling proposition (USP). When you cannot differentiate yourself on the basis of technical competence, the need for a USP becomes important. But what would happen if everyone had a USP? Do not worry about it. The state current of interviewing makes that unlikely. Your own well-articulated USPs will make you competitive in any interviewing process. One needs to think in terms of ways they have performed in the past with distinction and link those episodes to the job and organization to which they are applying.

A. YOU MUST GIVE A PERSON A REASON TO BUY YOUR PRODUCT
B. YOU MUST GIVE AN ORGANIZATION A REASON TO HIRE YOU

Only a few people in any organization can legitimately claim to make a difference. The opportunity to hire someone who can (think of our tiebreaker) will likely be too much to resist. That is why understanding the value one creates and learning how to talk about it are among the most important things one can do.

A. CLAIMS OF DIFFERENTIATION WITHOUT PROOF ARE JUST CLAIMS
B. CLAIMS OF CREATING VALUE WITHOUT PROOF ARE JUST CLAIMS

This is a real challenge. Many people work in bureaucracies that obfuscate responsibility and visibility. Inefficient organizations allow people to hide without having to create value. For example, many large (and not so large) American banks before consolidation were guilty of this. There are stories of banks consolidating and reducing head count only to find they were soon back or close to pre-merger head count numbers. The inability to control head count and get real productivity gains was a hangover from the postwar expansion days. Companies are just getting the knack of this. Meanwhile, people have been able to hide in and amongst the bureaucratic weeds without ever having been held accountable for productivity. That game is almost gone. The new skill requirement is one of creating value.

For the past three years I have participated on a panel sponsored by the Graduate School at Michigan State University. The purpose is to provide graduate students from all disciplines with career advice. The panel members have remained constant, and each year Rebecca Humphries, Director of the Michigan Department of Natural Resources gets asked the same question: What can someone just starting out do to distinguish oneself? Her answer has remained the same: "Find a task that needs doing and that no one else wants to do. Then do it with distinction." In other words, her advice is to differentiate yourself.

A. COMMUNICATE YOUR DIFFERENCE
B. COMMUNICATE YOUR DIFFERENCE

"Just as you cannot keep a light under a basket, you can't keep your difference under wraps. Every aspect of your communication should reflect your difference." Having a personal brand and learning to talk about it is something that needs to be done long before the interview. If you have not started, do so immediately. Starting now is better than waiting until later. It will only get easier and give you a greater advantage as you go along.

A few words need to be said about preparation and the actual interview process. The translation of interviewing into business terms is nothing more than selling. For many, the "s" word is difficult to swallow. Perhaps you have heard that human resources people in particular do not like to be sold to.

Marketing (brand management) and selling are not the same, but are closely related. Marketing is an attempt to predispose the buyer to buy. Selling is actually closing the deal. Having a good reputation (brand) no one buys makes the whole thing a rather moot point.

The overriding principle of most sales training is that great salesmen do not sell, they listen. No doubt, the reason people do not like being sold to is because someone on the other end misunderstands what it means to sell. Good selling is good listening because it helps one understand what is of importance to the organization with which you are interviewing. One can listen in a variety of ways—reading industry-related articles as well as company-specific material. But the major issues companies deal with are usually industry-related. For example, American-based airlines are all facing the same pressures, some better than others. The same is true of hospitals and the medical care industry in general. When going into an interview, it is important to understand what is of importance to the organization and how the people interviewing you see the issues. You can only get that by listening. If and when you hear something that relates to the value you create, you are in a position to bring it forward.

Another distinguishing characteristic of outstanding salesmen is their insistence on selling only features that are of interest to the buyer. Emphasizing remote automobile starting systems might be of interest in Minneapolis, but not in Miami. The only way you can find out is to listen. In this context it is helpful to find out why the position is open and what they hope to accomplish by filling it before you launch into the strengths you bring to the job.

Those concepts, in conjunction with references in the resource section, should send you on your way to greater value creation and interviewing experiences in an increasingly competitive world.

NEGOTIATION

Negotiating offers of employment is one of those areas in which the career transition industry has continued to be relevant. Some of this has to do with the reality that the rules of negotiation have not changed much over the years. It is the easiest of all the job placement processes because it happens at a point in time when the hard work of finding a job and getting an offer are already completed. However, do not be misled. Some parts of the process are tricky and when left in the hands of clumsy negotiators on either side can result in disaster. The Resources section is particularly useful here. For the moment, we will content ourselves with comments intended to sensitize one to potential difficulties as well as provide a basic understanding of how to approach an upcoming negotiation.

The first rule of negotiation is to understand it for what it is—a process in which an individual and organization seek mutually acceptable terms of employment without doing damage to the current or future state of their relationship. Unfortunately, both parties sometimes forget they are at a stage in which they agree on many more things than they disagree. When this happens, the tendency is to focus far too narrowly, thereby putting more stress on the relationship than it can reasonably be expected to bear.

You may have noticed that in high-stakes/high-level negotiations, people use agents to negotiate on their behalf rather than involve themselves directly. Occasionally high-profile people do their own negotiating. By and large, having a third party do it is a good idea. For one thing, it allows one to push the envelope without appearing to be unreasonable. The negotiator can more easily take the heat when unusual requests are made. Things are more easily positioned as trial balloons rather than intransigent demands. This should not be taken to mean that the negotiation process can, or should, be ceded entirely to a third party. It does mean that skillful third-party negotiators are used because they can make it easier to test the water on positions that might otherwise appear unreasonable. In addition, having a third party negotiate the sticky issues keeps contentiousness developed during the negotiating period from spilling over into the relationship once agreement is reached.

Third parties come into play most often when positions are being filled through a search firm. Because these firms are paid by the company, some may be reluctant to use them as their representative in a negotiation process.

After all, they owe their allegiance to who is paying the bill and not to the job applicant. Search consultants make excellent third-party negotiators. By the time a candidacy has gotten to the offer stage, the self-interest of the search consultant and applicant are closely aligned. Both want to close the deal if at all possible, neither wants to push the company beyond its comfort zone, and both want to get to an acceptable offer quickly. If certain issues become deal-breakers for either party, the consultant is an excellent intermediary for fielding those kinds of issues. He will let both parties know ahead of presenting the issue that it will likely push the envelope beyond what the other is willing to accept. Admittedly, the coincidence of self-interest between the applicant and search consultant is not perfect, but it is good enough to get most deals done.

Few employment negotiations are weighty enough to require a third party, leaving most people having to negotiate for themselves. But whether one has a third party or not, there are four areas one needs to be in-the-know about before entering a negotiation process. They are presented here with no consideration of relative importance save for the first one discussed. It is the most important of all.

Know what is important to you in a new job. Determining this well ahead of any job offer being made is critical. The very nature of the negotiating process can blur one's thinking and make one lose track of priorities as some things appear more important in the moment than they really are in the more normal course of things.

One way to see this is to make a list of fifteen things you want in a new job and write each one on its own 3x5 index card. Divide the cards into three piles of five each. The first five cards are the things you see as being most important; the next pile of five are labeled less important; and the last pile, least important. Once you have decided, put the list away and pull it out again when you are negotiating for a new position. As the offer unfolds, ask yourself how many of your "most important" items are a part of the employment value proposition being offered. Sometimes people accept positions that contain relatively few of the things they saw as important earlier in the process. That happens because people have difficulty focusing on what is important to them until actually confronted with the situation. At other times it happens because priorities change. Regardless, understanding how a new position fits with your personal priorities can help establish your list of things to negotiate. It can help you decide which things to concede and which to put down as absolute deal-breakers. Establishing your own priorities can be a helpful compass in the negotiating process.

Here is a typical list with which to experiment:

1. 401K program with at least a 25 percent employer match
2. 20 percent more salary than I currently make
3. Company-paid pension plan

4. No relocation
5. Grandfathered vacation time
6. Signing bonus
7. Bonus eligibility of at least 20 percent of salary
8. Flexible working hours
9. Emergency day care
10. Immediate eligibility for health care coverage
11. Workplace diversity
12. History of providing transition assistance for laid-off employees
13. No more than 20 percent travel
14. Formal career development program
15. Availability of fitness programs for employees

Know what is and what is not on the table. There are some things companies may not be in a position to do. For example, if their health care coverage has a waiting period, it is not something that can be waived on a selective basis without jeopardizing the tax status of the entire program. However, if you are eligible for COBRA coverage, they could *more* easily pay for that coverage until you have completed the waiting period. There are a variety of programs, benefits, and payment systems out there. Familiarize yourself with them to determine which may apply in your circumstance. If you do not know what is possible, there is a good chance you cannot negotiate it.

Know how you stack up against your competition for the position. This may not always be possible. Generally speaking, when you are first among many candidates that fit the bill, your chances to negotiate are diminished vis-à-vis situations in which you are the only viable candidate. Others are likely waiting in the wings. The *more* a candidate is one of a kind, the greater are his chances to negotiate. But unless one has highly reliable information, be cautious. Disaster lurks when an applicant believes himself to be one of a kind but is not.

Know the value you are expected to create for the organization. This is one of those areas in which context is everything. Business developers, especially in the consulting business, are taught to price their services according to the size of the problem they are expected to solve rather than the amount of time they spend solving it. The former calculation is always greater. This requires listening and careful positioning. The listening portion has to do with having the organization describe the problem they are trying to solve by filling the position for which you are a candidate. It is also learning about the costs to the company of having the position remain open or filled by the wrong person. At that point the consulting fee/salary offer is often considered a small price to pay for filling the position. Consultants try to avoid discussions about what organizations may have budgeted for consulting fees and instead focus on the cost of the status quo. Typical positions in organizations are confined by salary ranges and, for the most part, it is unrealistic to think they will wander beyond those constraints. It is reasonable, however, to get positioned toward the higher end of a salary range when viewed in the context of being the one candidate who can really create value.

What does any of this have to do with losing jobs to technology and globalization? Absolutely everything. We are in an age in which those just starting their career can, according to some, expect to change careers more times than their parents did. Very little of this is voluntary. Most of it is an outgrowth of megatrends and global forces impacting how work gets done as well as who does it. Since, changing jobs is something we all will likely do more of, it makes sense to develop the required skills.

Beyond that, we are in a time when the elements that constituted good jobs are eroding. Good jobs continue to exist, but there are fewer of them. Soon people in transition may be looking for jobs that are not there. Responsibility for funding our pensions and health care insurance continue to be shifted to the individual. Company-sponsored career development is a poor imitation of what it used to be. Job security is good only until the next merger, acquisition, or outsourcing deal.

Individuals just starting their careers and those in transition continue the search for safe companies with safe jobs. As people begin rotating through their third and fourth downsizing, two moods are emerging—one of brooding and anger, and another of opportunity and optimism. Often the difference in the two moods is not in skill set, but rather in the levels of understanding each has about the context in which work in America exists today.

CHAPTER EIGHT

❧❧

THE ENTREPRENEURIAL SPIRIT: A CASE STUDY

IT IS OVER three months into the transition process and Mary's group has jelled. They enjoy each other's company, and on days when their searches are slow seek out one another for support. Some occasionally have lunch or dinner together to share new developments or just to stay connected. Mary encouraged this from the very beginning because she knew they would need and appreciate the opportunity to be with others who share a common circumstance.

Dan Bowman is like most members of the group. He enjoys their company and is pleased that individual members are available to keep his spirits up. He has yet to miss a group meeting. But he is also ambivalent. He views his dependence as somewhat of a crutch and will be glad when he can associate with them because he wants to rather than because he needs to.

Dan hates being unemployed, and having someone tell him his services were no longer needed was personally repugnant. All his life he prided himself on being stubbornly self-reliant. His motto was "If you want something done right, do it yourself." When first told about his termination, he was angry at himself and his employer. His self-directed angst came from a personal sense of failure. The son of second-generation immigrant parents and the only one of three of children to attend college, he had always been held up as the "smart" one.

Dan's first job out of college was in the telecom industry, which gave him the opportunity to pursue his interest in computers. Eventually he headed up a group of software engineers who saw themselves as leading-edge. The unspoken word among his brothers (both licensed electricians) and their families was that Dan's example was the one to follow. Being unemployed and having it visible to his family added insult to injury.

He was angry at his company because this was not what he had signed up for. They promised him an opportunity to have a long-term career if he worked hard. Being downsized, outsourced, and let go were not a part of the deal or his vocabulary. Now, almost two decades after he started, these words had become a regular feature in the lives of everyone in the industry.

Dan found the job search process frustrating. He did not like the feeling of relying on others or being subject to forces beyond his control. He wanted a job that would give him his old sense of security. Yet he knew that even if he wrote the perfect résumé, became an expert connector, and found a great job, there was no assurance the same thing would not happen all over again. The ads he responded to increasingly characterized their jobs as stints rather than careers.

A couple of people in the group had job offers and were deciding whether to relocate their families or commute and return home on weekends. Commuting is sometimes easier than relocating teenage children in high school. Beside, they had all heard the horror stories about people relocating and shortly thereafter being let go.

From time to time Dan would think about how he had arrived at this place in his life. The world he knew—the one he grew up in and went to college to prepare for—had changed. Working in corporate America was no longer a path one could follow with reasonable assurance of security and advancement. Somehow big business was being run by people who have a different mind-set. He did not know what had happened or why. Sitting in the quiet of his home office, he thought how much better things would be if he were his own boss. "Maybe, just maybe, I should go into business for myself."

Mary started the next session of her group in typical fashion. "Does anyone have news to report or questions they want to pose for the group to consider?" Dan, seated in the rear of the room, rose and moved toward the front. On the way and in a louder than normal tone, he began addressing the group.

"As you know, I have not felt very positive about this whole situation. I keep thinking to myself how I worked hard for a company that ended up being poorly run. They continued to pour millions of dollars down one rat hole after another but the financials and stock price kept losing ground. After each investment fiasco, they would announce yet another round of job eliminations. At first I thought all I needed to do was keep my head down and work harder. It was like I was driven by some strange notion that my efforts would be recognized and no one would get rid of someone who contributed as much as I did. Even if they eliminated my job, they would want to keep someone with my credentials and productivity. As is now obvious, my job did get eliminated and so was my employment with the company."

By now Dan's voice filled every corner of the room—partly because of its elevated volume, but also because of the lack of competing noises. The group focused on what Dan was saying because they did not know where he was headed and because he was saying publicly what some of them had been thinking privately. There is a certain indignity that comes with losing one's job, and people were relieved to hear someone besides themselves come out with it.

Dan continued.

"What concerns me is that the jobs I have been applying for provide absolutely no assurance the same thing won't happen again. I am also not getting much of a response. While I do not believe software engineers are a dime a dozen, there seems to be an awful lot of them looking for work just now. A few weeks ago I saw an ad for a position I swear was written with me in mind. It fit me to a tee. Everything they were looking for, I had either done myself or managed a group that did it. So I applied. After I did not hear from them, I called. Boy, was I shocked. They said they had filled the job two weeks ago with someone from inside and only contacted those who had been invited in for interviews. So, not only did I not get the job, I didn't even get onto the candidate slate. Well, that was the last straw. My announcement to you today is that I intend to go into business for myself. I am looking to be my own boss. I am looking to make sure the only person who can fire me, or eliminate my job, or take my pension away, is me."

Dan was reasonably calm during his announcement, though there was an unmistakable intensity in his voice letting everyone know of his frustration. Until that moment they thought Dan was actively engaged in a search for a new position very much like the one he had before. He had gotten a couple of courtesy interviews but nothing came of them. He got close once, but after a seemingly endless interview process he came in second place. He was so focused on this one prospect that he stopped all other job search activities. His was a typical reaction. Looking for a job is uncomfortable and having a good prospect at hand is often the only excuse one needs to stop. Since "it ain't over 'til it's over," job-seekers are advised to maintain a steady level of activity through and until the search is successfully concluded. Some career consultants advise their clients that they should really never stop looking even though gainfully employed.

Mary had not gone that far, but had cautioned each member of the group to push themselves to continue searching, especially when it looked as if they were about to land a position. Many job offers fall through at the last moment, and if one stops looking, it is difficult to regain momentum.

Mary suspected Dan's announcement was as much the result of his frustration as it was a serious intent to start his own business. But she had seen this before and knew better than to engage him about it in front of the group. She could tell he needed a lot more information before moving forward. His lack of forethought, however, did not mean that becoming a business owner was necessarily a bad idea. Right now it was just an idea that was not well thought out.

Mary reminded the group of a previous topic they had covered about business start-ups and that while between jobs it is a good time to consider alternative career choices. Dan is like many Americans who dream of starting their own business. A recent survey conducted by Federal Express confirmed a full majority of Americans like the idea of starting a business. Mary's job now was to help him put the requisite thought and planning behind the idea. At the end of the group session, she asked him to meet with her in order to provide a list of resources he might find useful.

Other members of the group listened to the exchange between Dan and Mary with interest. Their collective intent seemed to be one of staying reasonably close to the situation to see if the entrepreneurial route might be appropriate for them. They were not quite so ready to announce any such intent as Dan had because they sensed that such an undertaking would be both difficult and risky. They were right.

It was a couple of days before Dan and Mary could arrange a mutually convenient time to meet. By then he had calmed down and tried to put more thought into what he had announced. He shared the idea with his wife, who was much more willing than Mary had been to ask challenging questions. "What kind of business? How much will it cost? Where will the money come from? Will it provide a steady income? What happens if the business fails?"

Of course, Dan had none of the answers. However, he was sure about a number of things. He had a lot of personal knowledge about computers, knew how they worked and how to stay current with the associated technology. He also sensed—but did not know for sure—that the home computer/home office market would stay hot for years to come. Dan's thought was to start a home computer consulting service to help people set up their computers and keep them free of viruses and other operating problems the average home computer owner could not easily handle. He was also sure he did not like the vulnerability he felt in this current condition of unemployment. Beyond sounding like a good idea and not liking the job search process, Dan knew little else.

He was, purposely, a few minutes late for his meeting with Mary to avoid running into other members of the group. He wanted to avoid the obvious questions they would ask simply because he did not have any of the answers, nor was he buoyed by the prospect of having others know he had made a public announcement without much forethought. As he approached Mary's office, he had the same twinge of anxiety he felt when the group first met. He had already been embarrassed by the paucity of answers to his wife's questions. He hoped the meeting with Mary would not be a repeat.

Mary's objectives and concerns about the meeting were different. She knew Dan's thoughts were not fully developed. Her objective was to challenge him without inviting discouragement. She had worked with numerous people on both ends of the business planning spectrum—those with well-reasoned approaches to becoming an entrepreneur as well as those who came to the conclusion very much the same way Dan had. Her sense was that it was far too early to predict either failure or success.

During the first hour of their meeting, Mary went into listen mode. She wanted to understand what Dan knew and did not know about being a business owner. She wanted to make sure he developed a good sense of the tasks at hand and how to get a handle on them. She thought it would be more effective for Dan to discover these for himself rather than taking them as gospel from her.

The meeting lasted a full two and a half hours, after which they agreed to withhold judgment on Dan's idea until he learned more. The first phase of that learning was to focus on whether he had the kind of personality profile required to strike out on his own. She also urged him to connect with people who had actually lived the entrepreneurial life in order to benefit from their experiences. Mary suggested he start with the Small Business Administration's website (www.sba.gov) and meet early the following week to review what he found.

Dan left Mary's office with a renewed sense of dedication. He was pleased not to have been embarrassed. "Perhaps," he thought to himself, "I wasn't so rash after all." He still did not have any more answers than he did before, but at least he had some idea of where to get them.

The next time they met, Dan's boyish enthusiasm was replaced by a compliant realism nurtured by what he had learned. On the one hand, he was pleasantly surprised to learn how much small business was a part of the American landscape. In any one year, they accounted for anywhere between 60 and 80 percent of new jobs. On the other hand, it was disturbing to find out that in the year in which there were over 550,000 start-ups, there were an alarming 584,500 failures (USSBA survey). Those numbers were supported by a Dunn & Bradstreet report which estimated that businesses with less than twenty employees have a 37 percent chance of surviving four years and only a 9 percent chance of making it to ten years. Another article pointed out that 50 percent of all start-up businesses fail in the first year and 95 percent fail in five years.[1] This was sobering news.

Mary's reaction to Dan's new realism was not that he should abandon the thought of starting a business. It was quite the opposite. Dan was obviously getting a much better grip on the situation and was more prepared than ever to proceed, albeit with caution. Mary had worked with many people who had the same information Dan had, but were unable to apply it to their situation. She encouraged him to continue with his research and begin connecting with people who had start-up experience.

At that point, Dan remembered Paige Stewart (one of the original members of the group), who had started her own advertising and marketing firm, which she gave up to become executive vice president of marketing for her largest (and only) client. As luck would have it, Paige was in the outplacement offices that day cleaning out her space and was able to spend time with Dan. She had just landed a senior position with an up-and-coming ad agency and was looking to help them reconnect with her previous employer. In addition, she was quite pleased with how things had worked out and was anxious to share news of her good fortune with others.

Dan was anxious to hear why Paige chose to go work for someone else rather than restart her own business. He thought some words of wisdom from someone who had been there could provide valuable insight into his own situation. Surprisingly, what he expected to hear from Paige—"starting a new business is just too difficult and risky," or, "It is easier to let someone else worry about the business"—was not a part of the conversation.

Paige had been contacted by the ad agency to help them land her prior employer as a client. Initially they wanted her to work for them on a project basis. She had maintained a good relationship with the new owners of her old firm and had been promised careful consideration if she chose to start her own agency again. She obviously knew the account well and would be a substantial asset to them. She also knew she would be right back in the same position as before—a small firm with a single account requiring 100 percent of her time. She walked Dan through the situation she faced as a single parent trying to build a successful business. She pointed out that her most significant mistake was misunderstanding the endgame.

"I mistook the job offer to come inside," observed Paige, "as a form of job security. They never told me, and I never thought to ask them, about their exit strategy from the business. Their intention all along was to develop the business to a certain point and let someone else provide the infusion of capital needed to take it to the next level. Their intent was to create value and cash out. When they first told me about selling the business, I felt betrayed. It took me a while to understand how skewed my feelings were."

Paige went on to explain how she went about developing a single-client relationship and took the lifeline they offered to become an employee. As near as she could tell now, the exit strategy was a longer-term proposition, but the business grew so fast, the opportunity to cash out came much sooner. "In retrospect," observed Paige, "the original owners had no way of knowing the acquiring company would have their own marketing executive and that my position would not exist going forward. Besides, they made the right decision. The other marketing person had more experience, had worked with them a long time, and was someone they trusted. Their decision was not a comment about me as much as it was a solid business decision any smart businessperson would make." Paige began talking about the "employment value proposition" she was offered to become the EVP of marketing. It was a relatively new term for Dan, but one he was hearing more and more. According to her, it was exactly what she had asked for and exactly what she needed—a steady, relatively secure income. She finally realized the rest of the assumptions she had about that job offer had come from an earlier time in her employment history and not from any promises they had explicitly made to her. She thought in terms of her career with the firm and the pension that would result. Of course, the pension was a 401K she put aside out of her wages with pretax dollars and a good match from the company. Dan interrupted, "How would knowing about their exit strategy have changed your decision to become the EVP of marketing?"

"I am not sure it would have changed it. But what I am sure about is those experiences changed what I am doing now."

"How so?"

Paige explained the proposition she put on the table when the ad agency approached her about coming to work on a project basis. She was sure she would be able to land the account, but wanted the relationship to be one of mutual benefit and risks. If they were willing to hire her as a full-time employee without signing a nonsolicitation/noncompete agreement, she would land the account within a year. If she didn't, they could terminate their employment relationship and she would be free to stay in the business with another firm or on her own. Both Paige and the owners of the ad agency knew she had the inside track on the account, and that landing it would put them over the top. They needed one another. In truth, Paige could land the account regardless of whether she worked for herself or someone else. The important variable was Paige, the value she created as a result of having the inside track and her personal brand in the market.

"The employment value proposition with my new employer," observed Paige, "is straightforward. They are betting on my background and previous connections to land a major account. In the process I am betting I can land that account, update my skills, develop new account relationships loyal to me, and generally get reconnected in the marketplace. If they want me to stay, I can. If I want to leave and start my own firm, I will. This mutual understanding of self-interest not only does not make either of us bad people, it also makes us appropriately informed about the employment value proposition we both require and need to honor. I, not my employer, am responsible for my career. I am the one who will have to pay for my children's college educations. I am responsible for creating a retirement fund. And I am responsible for looking out for me. I expect nothing less from them."

Dan was a little put off by Paige's singular focus on her own self-interest. That is not the way he had learned to conduct business. "What about loyalty and doing what is right because it is the right thing to do? What about the team you join? Is there no room for old-fashioned values?"

She came right back at him.

"I would hate to think that we live in a world in which there is no room for those things. There is and should be room. Having values and a moral compass is not an excuse for being fuzzy about mutual interests and the mutual commitments around those interests. Every day we hear of people being surprised about losing their jobs. The surprise comes because they thought working for a company was a long-term commitment. As it turns out, employers are reluctant to make those kinds of promises any more, implied or otherwise. We rely on our work to care for our families and provide a positive self-worth. I do not think it is unreasonable to understand what the commitment between you and your employer is and is not."

Dan ended his conversation with Paige slightly confused about her situation but less confused about his own. Until now, he had connected with others trying to find a job. There were times he wished people would just come right out with it. "Yes, I know of a job you can apply for" or, "No, I cannot help you." That seemed so simple and direct. He never quite understood why he was being counseled to dance around the subject. Now, after talking with Paige, he was pleased with how willing she had been to share information with him, as it was one of the most valuable connecting sessions he had ever had. He also noted that the conversation was not about a job lead.

Dan revisited the SBA website to take an assessment designed to determine if he had the personal characteristics required to become an entrepreneur. He initially put off taking it until he learned more about what it meant to be one's own boss. He had definitely matured in his thinking and saw that it was about time he got more realistic about this whole thing. He knew if he did not have the inclination or talent to own a business, the rest of what he was thinking did not really matter. He saw himself as being at a go/no-go step in the process. If it was no-go, he needed to get cracking right away looking for that next job.

The SBA assessment is a series of twenty-five questions, each of which could be answered "yes," "maybe," or "no." The questions asked for responses on topics such as persistence, willingness to take chances, and the desire to control one's own fate. The assessment was scored online and provided immediate feedback. Before getting his final score, however, Dan asked his wife to review each answer to see if she agreed with his assessment of himself. In his mind, this was no time for anything less than brutal honesty. He knew that the accuracy of the assessment would depend on the quality of his assessment of himself.

With minor exceptions, they agreed. There were four categories of scores: 1. ready to start your own business; 2. high potential, but need to improve skills or hire someone with those skills; 3. do not start a business alone; and, 4. self-employment may not be for you. Dan scored at the low end of "high potential" but just above "Do not start a business alone."

He met again with Mary to share the mixed results of his research and connecting. He told her about his meeting with Paige and how exciting it had been to see things in a different light. He learned a lot and began to understand why connecting with people for information might be more productive than asking if they knew of job openings. People are often happy to give what they can. Asking them for the benefit of their experiences or advice will likely yield better results. If that was the good news, the not-so-good news was Dan's score on the assessment.

As always, Mary's demeanor did not change when she heard about Dan's score and meeting with Paige. She asked what he thought the assessment meant.

"It probably means I need to do some additional research."

"Good idea."

They both agreed that taking a closer look at the research on small business failures would be a good place to start. She referred him to several publications and again to the SBA website, where Dan was able to locate a book by

Michael Ames entitled *Small Business Management*.[2] In his book, Ames identifies many reasons why small businesses have high failure rates, including:

- Lack of experience
- Insufficient capital
- Poor location
- Overinvestment in fixed assets
- Poor credit arrangements
- Personal use of funds
- Unexpected growth

Other publications had different lists, but they were all pretty much alike. Dan felt himself growing in his level of sophistication. Though still without many of the answers, he was beginning at least to ask the right questions. He was also struck by the number of variables that could negatively impact the odds of a business succeeding, including the very success of the business itself— unexpected growth. These are things about which he had never given a moment's thought. Because he knew so little and there was so much to learn, he was beginning to think that starting his own business might be nothing more than a pipe dream. It was then he came across one of the most unusual articles he had read, "Using Goldratt's Thinking Process to Improve the Success Rate of Small Business Start-Ups." Though complicated and written in an unusual style, he understood just enough to begin applying it to his own situation.

Dan was impressed by the statement that "in order to maximize the system production [Dan saw this to mean the process by which he was making the decision to start a business], the slowest process must be improved and all other processes regulated to the speed of the slowest." This helped Dan see his decision-making as a series of interrelated/mutually dependent steps. If any one of them was not implemented fully, it could jeopardize the entire process regardless of how well thought out and implemented the others were. The article highlighted a critical thinking process whereby one could both anticipate the consequences of a poorly executed step as well as create an interjection to reduce that step's impact. In other words, starting up a business had at least two major prerequisite components: figuring out what one does not know or cannot control effectively (the risks), and then deciding what to do about them. Finally, Dan figured out he had been asking questions in the wrong sequence. His opening question always had been, should he go into business for himself? He should have asked, what it would take to go into business? It is the answer to this latter question that drives the answer to the first. If the answer is, it will not take much because he has the resources, experience, favorable market conditions, and so on, then it is a straight path to going into business with a reasonable chance of being successful. Asking what it takes leads to a research path and a connectivity scheme aimed at getting answers and managing results (risks).

Dan's next meeting with Mary was qualitatively different from the others. With a determined calmness, he advised her, "I've figured some of this out. The question is: What will it take for me to open my own business? The answer is, I don't quite know, but I sure as hell will find out."

Over the next couple of months Dan was a whirling dervish of activity. He broadened his research and connecting activities to deal with the multitude of things he did not know about starting his own business.

He needed to know more about the industry. He discovered that a lot of people were getting into the home computer business, one way or another. Much of the help desk and online parts of the business were being outsourced/ offshored, which provided the dual advantage of lower costs and 24/7 operations because of the different time zones. It also seemed to be a fragmented industry troubled by ease of entry and difficulty with quality control and costs. Dan's initial thinking was some of that could be controlled by offshoring. He began visiting with people who were hands-on in the industry to exchange ideas and identify risks. He was pleased and surprised at the willingness of people to share information and give advice. Mary's advice about connecting was beginning to make sense to him.

He needed help with a business plan. Dan joined a group of would-be entrepreneurs who met biweekly to discuss everything from financing to business planning. There he learned of the tremendous number of books available on the subject (see Resources section). He quickly understood that some approaches to business planning were better than others. He also discovered that a significant number of people were there to get help putting a plan together because a lending agency required it and not because they were looking for a road map to success and growth. How strange, he thought, that people would assume that a bank's interest in financing their venture would be perfectly coincident with their own. Dan's thought was that he would rather have a plan he could use and that others would find worth investing in rather than a plan the bank found acceptable but might be of marginal use to him.

He needed help with personnel management. Dan was aware of the online courses offered by the SBA, so he enrolled. He also understood that his timing and needs might be more immediate than the courses would allow. He kicked himself for not thinking of the course route sooner, but still was willing to use it to improve his overall business background and acumen.

He needed help with financing. He began to explore different financing arrangements available to get himself up and running. Again surprises were in store. Venture capitalists, by and large, were asking for guaranteed annual returns and, failing that, the right to sell the business to get what they could on the open market.

Banks were largely uninterested in such ventures and were more risk-adverse than he had ever imagined. He also learned about something called "angel" investors, but they seemed to want a lot of say-so about the day-to-day operations of the business.

The list of things was longer than Dan had anticipated. Even though he had connected individually with more than forty people and had received some solid advice, he still felt uneasy about taking the final leap. However, the business plan was coming together and he had developed some ideas about financing that would give his personal funds less exposure and his wife more comfort.

At one of his networking group sessions, Dan was approached by one of the members about the possibility of becoming a franchisee. Of course, he knew about franchising but had never really thought seriously about it. Intrigued, he wanted to hear more. His research did not surprise him this time. From a risk perspective, franchise opportunities ran the gambit. Generally speaking, the greater the risk to the franchisee, the easier it is to get in. Highly stable franchises with demonstrated returns require a greater initial investment of capital and come with more restrictive entrance requirements. Having this knowledge was good news because it allowed him to regulate his risk exposure up front. He was flattered about being approached and promised to look into it in more detail. More than that however, Dan was beginning to understand. And, the more he understood, the more he was able to take control.

It had been quite a couple of months for Dan. He was putting the finishing touches on his plans to open a business and was actively considering becoming a franchisee. The two processes were similar enough to be planned in tandem.

That evening Dan got an interesting telephone call from one of his connections, Rebecca Epstein, who wanted to see him the next day. As there seemed to be a sense of urgency, he agreed. Dan had learned that job-hunting and career planning are lonely businesses. He knew that being responsive to someone he had connected with would be appreciated.

Times had changed. Initially Dan did all the calling and was a net importer of information. Now it was more common for people to call him for the same kind of connecting information and advice he had been asking for only a few months earlier. Regardless of whether Dan made the call or someone called him, he still found these sessions informative and useful. It was a source of pride that he had established enough of a reputation (personal brand) to be sought out.

The next day Dan met with Rebecca and got a surprise. He was becoming well known in certain circles for being knowledgeable about the help desk business, and more than a few people saw him as a real comer. The call and follow-up meeting was a job offer from a start-up company similar to but not exactly like the one he was contemplating starting. Rebecca did have a home computer service business she wanted him to run along with all of the operations. The salary was comparable to what he was making before and there were plenty of stock options to make success in the business attractive. Dan was elated and confused at the same time. When he was looking for a job, he could not get the time of day. All of a sudden, he has a start-up business plan, a franchise opportunity, and a job offer. Wow! He needed to meet with Mary.

The meeting was shorter than expected. As had always been the case, Mary was nonjudgmental and knew exactly what questions to ask.

"Dan, what is the endgame?" she asked.

"I still want to go into business for myself."

"What will it take?"

"Probably more knowledge than I have now, but I am worried that if not now, then when? But I don't want to be one of those who couldn't last a year, or five or ten. My endgame is to manage the risks in a way that maximizes my future chances for success."

He left Mary's office knowing that he had the answers to all his questions. After discussing it with his wife, he called Rebecca and accepted the job, but on one condition. He would have access to all phases of the operation, including the finances. He wanted to understand what it took to run the company so that he would be able to someday run his own. They immediately struck an agreement. The company got a dedicated employee anxious to learn about all facets of the business. They could not do much better than hire someone interested in the success of the business and willing to put in the time to learn it from stem to stern. They got someone interested in coming to work not just to get a paycheck but to make a difference. Likewise, Dan got a lot of what he wanted and needed. He had the time and opportunity to fill in some of those gaps about the business ownership without the associated risks. From the perspective of career management, Dan was managing his own career with the active complicity of his employer.

Over the course of the next three years, Dan spent time learning every detail of the business. He did not know everything about it, but he knew more than anyone else and gained a thorough understanding of what it would take to run the entire operation if he had to. Then one day Rebecca called her senior team together to announce she had gotten an offer for the business and was inclined to accept it. A few weeks later an announcement to all employees went out as follows: "We are pleased to announce the firm has been sold to . . ." Some employees had been through this before while others had only read about it. Being acquired meant consolidation and job elimination. In the meanwhile, individual productivity would drop as employees spent more time talking and worrying about their jobs than doing them. Dan, of course, was neither shocked nor dismayed. Beginning three years ago he took responsibility for his own career and knowledge about the industry. He had made a lot of good contacts and his future did not rely on Rebecca or anyone else providing him with a good job. He felt good about where he was and what he wanted to do. He took advantage of the advanced warning Rebecca had given senior management and began working on the business plan he had started three years before. As he read through his initial proposal, he was struck by how much the industry had changed in the interim and by how much more he knew about it. There were still a number of things he would need help with, but they were not as critically important this time. He knew the fundamentals of the business, where the new opportunities were, and what was needed to get a new business started. Dan also knew the employees well enough to know which ones he would be interested in recruiting to work with him. He was confident that any who lost their position to consolidation would make a good employee for him because he had been directly involved in hiring most of them.

When Dan walked his wife through his business plan, she did not raise any of the questions she had asked three years before. Instead she asked him, "What would it take to go into business for yourself?"

He responded, "Not very much. Not very much at all."

CASE STUDY EPILOGUE

For some people, having their company merged or their job outsourced is a devastating experience. It need not be. More than ever it is important to assume personal responsibility for your career and future. That can be done in many instances by learning to create value for oneself and for one's company. There perhaps will never be a full guarantee that the future will be secure. But it is possible to create better probabilities of things working to one's advantage. Dan figured *out* how to mesh the interests of his company with those of his *own* in a way that created mutual advantage. I made Dan's agenda more visible and transparent than it was in real life simply to get the points across. In reality, it may not be a good idea to be quite as *open* as Dan was. But in today's global world it is important to take control. The process of doing that will often allow one to create more value.

How one goes about learning how to create value depends very much on the situation. It is, as Einstein would say, relative. How that is so and what specifically you might do about it is covered in the next chapter.

How Some Entrepreneurs Got Started

A natural connector lands on his feet. I recently had lunch with a friend who used to be between jobs (code for *out of* . . . oh yes, but you know that now). I asked him to give me the details of how he landed this new situation as I wanted to share them with my readers. Here is what he told me. About a year ago he was summoned to the CEO's office and told that they wanted him to take another assignment. No, this was not a promotion. It was more of a lateral move than anything else. The CEO made no attempt to sugarcoat the message. They wanted to make a change for two reasons. First, the company had experienced unprecedented growth and he was needed to help integrate the various sales forces into a single unit, and no one was better positioned to manage that task than he. But second and more important, they needed to unblock his position in order to move a candidate forward who had been identified in the succession planning process. Bob (not his real name) described this meeting as the absolute worst of his entire career. He had been with the company for over thirty years and had risen to vice president of sales without a college degree. He was an officer of the firm and a loyal employee in good standing. His first reaction was one of anger. He advised the chairman that this move needed to be undone or it might not work for him at all. In retrospect, Bob was not quite sure what he meant by that statement, but he did know his level of anger was unlikely to subside anytime soon.

Given no other alternative, Bob tried the new job but could not make a go of it. "My heart just wasn't in it," he told me. A few months later he approached the chairman and asked if he could get a package to leave the organization. The chairman's response was, "Let me see if I understand you. You want me to pay you to leave, right?" Somewhat to his surprise, Bob was told of the organization's unwillingness to establish a pay-for-leaving precedent. But if he would be willing to time his exit with a more general reorganization, he could be covered under the company's rather generous job elimination policy. The deal was cut and Bob left within six months. Another six months and a couple of job offers later, Bob became a partner in a manufacturer's representatives business. When Bob was VP of sales, he had come in contact with the current owner. It was a perfect fit and a perfect deal. At the end of two years the contract called for Bob to buy out the current owner of the business at a multiple of annual sales, which could be generated from current business growth. Within a few months Bob landed his old company as an account that had substantial potential for growth. The details of how Bob got to a new situation so quickly have relevance for those who might be similarly situated.

Bob had been a connector all his life and had an extensive list of friends and associates to call on once he was in the job market. He quickly put together a list of forty "friends of Bob" who he thought might be in a position to give him advice and counsel about what he might do next. As he mentioned, this was not a list of his closest friends. In fact, most of them were on the list because of what they had to offer and not because of strong personal ties.

Before meeting with any of them, he worked through some ideas he thought made sense and subdivided them into A, B, and C priority groups. The groupings were based on the value he thought each could be to him and not on the strength of his personal relationships. He knew if he got two or three names from each meeting and followed up and got the same from their referrals and so on, the list would quickly mushroom out of control.

In each instance he was careful to let people know he was looking for their advice and counsel and not a job. He found all of them extremely supportive. Bob also made sure he continued to speak well of the company and showed no outward anger at what had happened. He still did not like what had happened, but he learned to live with it. An amiable departure made it easier to get good references. After all, he had poured his heart and soul into that company for over thirty years and did do a good job for them. Why complicate it with hard feelings and saying things he might regret?

Bob also understood what he wanted at this stage in his career. That led him to reject an opportunity in mainland China as well as one working with college professors to help bring their inventions to market. Incidentally, both of these offers were developed through his old company.

There were many more details. However, the main point is this: After being with the same company for thirty years and without a college degree, Bob's brand in the marketplace was strong enough to uncover good opportunities. Not all of us can take control as quickly as Bob did. Nor do all of us have personal brands as strong as his. But wherever we are along the journey—still employed, unemployed and looking, or knowing a person who is—now is a good time to take control of your brand. One thing is certain: Change will happen. The only question is, what are you going to do about it?

An exit strategy backfires—upward. One of my friends told me about some clients he had a few years ago, all from the same lending institution. Their company was purchased by an East Coast bank that had no apparent need for any of their talents. Rather than look for a new company to work for, they decided to start their own sub–prime lending institution. Their objectives were specific and limited. Five years and about $5 million net for each of the three would be all they would need for retirement. They started with $12 million in assets and developed an extensive and (they thought) airtight business plan. Rather than go into a business in which they had no experience, they choose to stick with what they knew. Chances of success are much better in these circumstances.

Everything seemed to work but their retirements. The business got so big and they got so wealthy, retirement has been all but impossible. "Last month alone," according to my friend, "they let out $2 billion in loans."

Family ties. One of my favorite stories is one in which I was involved personally. A human resources executive from a very large company had been let go and was having one heck of a time getting traction in the market. Late one evening after everyone had long since gone home, he and I were having one of those quiet chats that happen on occasion. As we both unwound ourselves from the day, the conversation strayed from one subject to another. We started talking about his only son and the difficulty the kid was having in school. He had been a poor student in high school and was now trying college just to "get his old man off his back." That of course ended in expended funds and nothing close to a degree. George (not his real name) wondered if the poor relationship he had developed with his son after years of arguing about school could be repaired. He had gotten a college degree and had a successful business career, all with one company. And now where was he? At the end of his career, out of work with no job prospects in sight, and having a bad relationship with his son.

The conversation with George did not last much longer, but I could see a visible change had come over him. I was concerned that our conversation had somehow crossed the line into an area of George's psychological makeup that I was unprepared to deal with.

A few months later I bumped into George at a local gas station. He thanked me for the conversation and said it had helped him finally figure something out.

"I needed to quit asking my son to be like me and accept him on his own terms. I called him after we talked and apologized for too many years of looking at things from the perspective of my ego and not his well-being. This started a discussion about things we were both good at. That was one hell of a surprise. We're going into the drapery business together."

I did not speak with George much after that and am almost afraid to ask how they are doing. But I do know that the meaning George can find in his new work can be greater than any he has ever experienced.

CHAPTER NINE

❧✦

SUGGESTIONS FOR SURVIVAL AND PROSPERITY

ONE OF THE central themes of this book is that jobs and careers continue to be important. How they are managed, however, has been changed by global forces on the scale of an industrial revolution. Nothing like this has gone before, as China and India are emerging as economic powers that will compete with the United States and Europe for the world's natural resources.

We have adjusted to change before. But those previous adjustments will seem easier than the ones called for now. The employment value propositions accompanying these transitions were developed against a backdrop of a war for talent. Health care insurance, career development, and pension programs became the organizational constructs around which Americans went to work and structured their lives.

In the 1970s companies began rethinking the employee value propositions needed in order for them to compete on a rapidly evolving global stage. Initially many did not know what to make of the changes in the rules by which they worked for their employers. In a sense, my father-in-law Roy and I went through this change together as we discussed different ways of handling redundant white-collar workers. Our interpretation relied heavily on a good-guy/bad-guy analysis that kept us from seeing broader forces at work.

As new employment value propositions emerged, they were reinforced by developments in technology. Productivity gains of mind-boggling proportion became possible as work increasingly involved the manipulation of data rather than of things. The gross national product (GNP) shifted dramatically from the cost of goods sold (steel, iron, and refrigerators) to the cost of goods and services, including software, x-ray readings, and consulting.

As distance dies, questions are raised. In a world in which those of European descent are a distinct minority and women are a clear majority, to what extent will race and gender continue as important considerations? Can the United States, or any nation that seeks to be competitive on a global stage, afford a suboptimal utilization of major segments of its population? Some things are becoming clearer: Race and gender continue to be relevant but are likely to be less so going forward. Having talent and getting results will become more important. The leveling of the global economic playing field places a premium on recognizing and using talent. Worldviews and patterns of thought interfering with those processes give advantage to smarter companies with smarter ways of operating.

Worldviews and the context they create also affect what people look for as they plan careers and conduct job searches. We are in a period of transition in which people continue to think in terms of the kinds of jobs they held in the past. Meanwhile, corporations have moved on. Sometimes their language is the same as it used to be—"join our firm and have a great career"—but the content and meaning of their messages have changed. What is meant by a career often has none of the elements of the good jobs for which we currently search. This undoubtedly creates confusion because there is a mismatch in the marketplace between what individuals are hearing and what companies are actually committing to as they employ new workers. Unfortunately, the mismatch is not as obvious as it needs to be.

We need to rethink the job search and career planning processes developed during the early years of the outplacement industry. Misunderstanding what corporations now mean as they advertise their careers will likely lead to frustration and feelings of having been let down by false promises of yet another employer. How we construct our résumés, connect ourselves to the marketplace of jobs, and otherwise manage our careers needs revision.

Getting to a different mind-set is facilitated by understanding what futurists are saying and how they work. What futurists really do is predict the past. That is, rather than look into a crystal ball to guess the future, they look at what has already happened and make educated guesses about how their observations will continue to show up tomorrow and perhaps decades later. Looking backward at some of the adjustments that institutions and companies have already made will facilitate our understanding of the corresponding adjustments that individuals will need to make in order to keep up. Institutional adjustments tend to represent a kind of collective best thinking in response to important changes in the environment. Generally, institutions do not change unless there is ample evidence that it is necessary. Otherwise the sheer weight of institutional inertia will force bureaucracies along their traditional paths.

While there is no guarantee that the institutions we choose to examine offer the best and most appropriate insight, the subject matter fueling their responses confirms what individuals are likely to be adjusting to and the direction those adjustments will likely take. Had this same reasoning been applied to the postwar competition for white-collar workers, we would have noticed changes in corporate behavior in the kinds of people being recruited and value propositions used to retain them. Those retention strategies were part of a mind-set shift about the value of a college education, which in turn sent Americans to college in unprecedented numbers. By taking a closer look at some of the institutional adjustments currently under way, we can also get a look at the factors influencing individual career choices and outcomes.

INSTITUTIONAL ADJUSTMENTS

One such institutional adjustment is happening in the Undergraduate Engineering Department at Northwestern University. According to Associate Dean Stephen Carr, recent trends in the employment of engineering graduates have forced significant adjustments in the department's curriculum. Now, about one-third of their graduating students land jobs with a significant offshore component. While most do not have to relocate to other countries, they can expect either to live abroad for as long as six months or have significant international travel during their initial employment period.

Another trend is related to salaries, which continue to rise but are no longer being set solely in the United States. Increasingly, job offers to American-based undergraduate engineers are established by offshore forces and organizations. One implication of this is a greater reliance on global markets in establishing supply and demand dynamics for graduating engineers.

The most startling development is the advice from the department to students that their first jobs out of college will last an average of no more than four or five years. After that, they will likely join the ever-growing list of people who for one reason or another are in transition. When asked whether students were insecure about the prospects of accepting temporary offers of employment, Dean Carr responded "they are less insecure and more anxious because they are moving into a world that has not been characterized for them."[1] This is a world with unfamiliar employee value propositions. These are not the good jobs their parents sought and they do not have the traditional elements students have learned to look for. Northwestern is beginning to adjust its curriculum in order to provide insight into what individuals will find useful in navigating the new economy. They have taken the forceful step of redefining the discipline of engineering itself. To them it is no longer a set of established, isolated processes through which things in the physical world are built. Instead, it is the "art of creating new things to improve peoples' lives." Carr refers to this new definition as a beginning in a shift of "habits of the mind" in which the traditional engineering curriculum is given a different context in which to exist.[2] It is a context that enhances the ability of its graduates to create value and thereby improve employability across a variety of circumstances.

Several correlations follow. First, students are advised to find places where value needs to be added. This is fostered by the establishment of an interdisciplinary focus for incoming students who learn to understand the broader context in which traditional engineering projects are conceived and completed. The perfect bridge has little value without its most perfect uses for people. Learning to look for places where value needs to be added helps students find and choose correspondingly appropriate places of work. They are taught that neither knowledge nor expertise (expertise is defined as the application of knowledge) is sufficient for success. They learn the importance of having *adaptable expertise* in order to reach the heights they set for themselves and their careers. It is an expertise that can be applied across multiple domains.

Dean Carr's sentiments were reinforced by Ed Colgate, PhD, director of Northwestern's Institute for Design Engineering and Application. His view is that technical skills have little to do with whether engineers fail or succeed. "They all have good technical skills." Engineers as well as others fail because they miss their targets. That is, engineering is a needs-driven process in which the engineer must understand who the stakeholders are in addition to stakeholder needs. Outstanding technical skills no longer differentiate students. The differentiators tend to be skills around customer focus, communication, and teamwork.[3]

By now the theme should be familiar. The employment value proposition has changed. People can expect to be hired, retained, and compensated on their ability to create value. The engineer whose job goes away after a few years can either be taught to expect that to happen or not. Those who understand the nature of jobs today are likely to be better prepared and positioned to manage their careers and job transitions. Those who do not understand will continue to wonder if there are any good jobs left.

Michigan State University (MSU) is another example of an institution responding to its changing context. It is doing so by making a dramatic clarification of its mission as a land grant institution. MSU is one of several large universities in the United States enabled by the Morrill Act of 1862, which stipulated the establishment of:

> at least one college where the leading object shall be, without excluding other scientific and classical studies and including military tactics, to teach such branches of learning as are related to agriculture and the mechanical arts.[4]

For more than a hundred years after its founding, MSU's image in the public mind had to do with agriculture and the extension of related principles to the state's agricultural community. Today MSU has grown to be one of the top 100 research universities in the world. Maintaining its position will require a funding configuration and rationale that are different from what has traditionally existed. The university has relied heavily on state funding. The state in turn has relied on the automobile industry, which continues to offshore its operations to stay competitive. DaimlerChrysler has recently called for more automobiles to be assembled in China, where workers earn $1.50 an hour compared with $49.50 in Germany. Delphi, the largest auto parts supplier in the United States and spun off by General Motors in 1999, has filed for bankruptcy. The speculation is that its future depends on its ability to reduce labor costs from current levels of $65 per hour ($27 in direct wages plus $38 in benefit costs) to $25 per hour. In 2005, Delphi's pension plans were reported to be underfunded by $10.8 billion, more than twice what was reported in 2004.[5] If Delphi cannot adjust its costs, it will likely cease to exist. If it can adjust, several things follow. Retirees will be poorer; jobs that once paid $65 an hour will be replaced by ones paying a lot less; and the middle-class existence of Delphi employees will be threatened. The ability of the state of Michigan to fund its institutions of higher education will continue to be severely challenged.

This is not new news for MSU (and other state-funded entities) since they have transitioned over the past fifteen years from being state-supported to state-assisted, as the proportion of its budget supplied by state funding dropped from 80 to 41 percent.

How far state funding will slip is unclear. What is clear, however is that MSU's continued survival as one of the world's top research universities will rely heavily on its ability to replace and exceed the shortfall created by declining state funding. Toward that end, and under the direction of its new president, Dr. Lou Anna Simon, MSU has taken some aggressive steps to clarify and restate its mission.

In a speech delivered on February 11, 2005, she noted, "I am not speaking here of the establishment of agricultural colleges, which many people mistakenly believe the land grant tradition to mean." The role Dr. Simon has in mind for MSU is one of practical relevancy to the aspirations and careers of people on a worldwide basis.

> As we focus on preparing Michigan—and the world—for the new economy, we must also take a look at today's students and the resources they will need to survive and to thrive in the decades ahead.
>
> They will need state-of-the-art knowledge to shape and advance their chosen careers. And, in the knowledge economy, they will need more—a whole new worldview, a new expectation of what applying that knowledge and developing a satisfying productive life will take.[6]

MSU characterizes its approach as "Boldness by Design," and at a time when its traditional funding sources are under siege, the university has reached out to embrace the new economy. It is an institution staring down the sources of its funding difficulties—global competition in the automotive industry and the redistribution of manufacturing capacity worldwide to more economically rational locations. It is a mission whose relevancy and value creation is defined by the newly emerging context of higher education not only in the state of Michigan, but also in the entire world. In the final analysis, a broader mission translates to a broader base on which to create value and from which to secure funding.

Corporations, not-for-profit institutions, and individuals are finding it necessary to redefine themselves in order to create value and survive. In the case of corporations like GM, surviving sometimes means eliminating entire classes of employees whose work is best done elsewhere or not at all. In the case of not-for-profit institutions, it means adjusting to the requirements of the new economy in creative ways others will find of value.

Any of us can choose to ignore the implications of the new economy, but only if we are willing to jeopardize our futures. Individuals, like institutions, will need to change. The only question is what direction should change take?

Peter Cappelli in *The New Deal at Work* concluded that "the old employment system of secure lifetime jobs with predictable advances and stable pay is dead."[7] Significantly, it was not a death that came at the hands of single-minded greedy business executives who would violate any rule of human decency in exchange for better profits. For what it is worth, Jack Welch was uncomfortable with his "Neutron Jack" label. Instead, he preferred for people to understand that he was dealing with a company so bloated in size that it posed a threat to GE's economic future. It is doubtful that executives at GM enjoy terminating people. They, like others, have responded to a rapidly evolving world in need of a new employment value proposition. Today's American-based corporations exist within a context that has changed. They are now quicker to adjust, but appear still somewhat reluctant. Cappelli observed:

> Senior management was made to feel guilty about breaking the old deal, and between 1996 and '97 almost half of US employers produced written material outlining new deals for their employees . . . the vast majority, 84 percent, reported that their policies and actions conveyed the essence of a new contract to the workforce . . . with General Electric's being typical:
> On job security: the only job security is a successful business.
> On loyalty: If loyalty means that this company will ignore poor performance, then loyalty is off the table.[8]

TOMORROW AND OUR MOST RECENT PAST

According to those good at predicting the past, the die has been cast, and there are a number of things happening today that we can expect to continue in a way that will define the adjustments individuals need to make to survive.

Offshore outsourcing as a primary means of controlling costs and risks will likely continue indefinitely into the future. To the extent that global competitors create industry best practices by moving operations, their efficiencies will have to be matched by other companies that will otherwise risk losing significant market share. Countries that can redeploy their workforces will have an advantage over those for whom redeployment is difficult. As globalization takes hold, agitation for more substantial safety nets will emerge. The debate need not, however, be positioned as safety nets versus no safety nets. Rather, careful attention will need to be given to improving worker security and simultaneously preserving the ability of countries to redeploy their work-forces to more profitable and cost-effective activity.

This position does not extend to having American corporations abandon the number of things they often are compelled to do under the banner of corporate citizenship. Nor is there any suggestion that the tax codes be altered in a way that provides disincentives to corporations.

In addition, the context in which decisions are being made about excess workers has changed dramatically and decisively from the time Humble Oil used job search counselors to redeploy relatively small numbers of its white-collar workers. Today's context gives greater permission and has allowed companies to issue new employment value propositions to their recruits and employees alike. Individual workers have been slow to recognize the change.

The use of temporary employees and the temp agency business is ample evidence of the evolving nature of the employment value proposition. It is now common for workers to be hired through third parties who agree to supply workers in response to variations in workload. As demand declines, companies are able to reduce their payrolls without being required to fulfill any of the commonly accepted functions associated with socially responsible downsizing activity. Unemployment and other insurance benefits do not have to be extended. As a result, the use of a contingent workforce is often less costly, and the flexibility companies gain in their ability to staff up and down quickly has substantial advantages.

At one time temporary employees were largely nonexempt clericals. The market has shifted to include white-collar professionals of all types as well as the more general level of management provided in the executive ranks. Hospitals and other health care organizations have been known to hire CEOs on a contingent basis until a permanent replacement can be located. In addition, many of the traditional staff positions in accounting, human resources, and legal lend themselves to contingent workforce arrangements.

An erosion of benefits is also likely to continue unabated. The most significant gap exists for those workers who may want or need to retire before the age at which they are covered by Medicare or who are no longer employed. The combination of the lack of retiree health care and access to affordable health care insurance forces many who are out of work into a high-stakes game of coverage. That is, they cannot afford insurance at the very time they cannot afford to have serious health issues.

In addition, employers will continue to pass increased health care cost back to employees through higher premiums and/or lower levels of coverage. Wal-Mart, McDonald's, Lowe's, Avis, and numerous others make limited benefit policies available, mainly to lower-level, part-time employees. While the premiums are generally affordable, the plans pay sometimes as little as $1,000 toward medical expenses. They are also among the fastest-growing health insurance offerings in the American workplace according to Chad Terhune, staff reporter for the *Wall Street Journal*. Companies tend to justify these offerings under the rationale that "some coverage is better than none."[9] Their less generous critics see them as another form of corporate exploitation. They are continued evidence of the ongoing erosion of benefit coverage in America as well as the effort on the part of corporations to control costs.

At the moment the cost advantages of limited benefit plans are confined to the working poor. The underlying economic rationale, though, is applicable to all. That is, the context in which health care benefits were extended to American workers has changed. Once a tool for attracting and retaining employees, they are now viewed more and more as a rising cost threatening returns on capital. Consequently, companies are looking to reduce their expenses and are beginning to question the appropriateness of an employer-based system.

Companies are controlling their costs by shifting them to customers and employees; by hiring classes of workers (temps/contingent) who may otherwise be ineligible for coverage; and ultimately by shifting production to areas of the world where costs are less onerous. In this respect the employer-based/AMA-approved system of rationing health care on the basis of ability to pay is on a collision course with emerging national priorities. Until resolved, many people are left without coverage because they do not have jobs. They are buffeted about by a system whose focus is on profitability and not health care. It is a system that distributes coverage to people when they need it least and keeps them from it when they need it most.

Career development issues may have less visibility than health care, but they are of critical importance. In the new economy the ability to create value is the personal currency for career advancement. That in turn relies heavily on the ability to keep one's skills updated and adaptable to new circumstances. Traditionally, employees received the necessary skills upgrades from their employers. Employer commitment to training has declined, with no discernible public policy in place that enables transitioning employees to retool. In this way the United States has only one side of the equation in hand: That is, employers are relatively free to redeploy workers, but there is nothing available in the way of public policy to facilitate development of the skills of those being redeployed.

Cappelli spoke of this when he noted:

> Under the new deal at work, employees have less job security; the attachment between employer and employee has weakened; leading to reduced incentives for employer training; new systems of work organization make internal development of employees more difficult; and compensation systems are increasingly driven by the outside market.[10]

When today's graduate engineers are forced to reenter the job market in five years, it will be important that their skills be current. This will be less likely to result from employer-sponsored training and development. Instead, the quality of their skills will be more a function of the mind-set with which they entered the workforce initially. It will come from having attended a school of engineering that emphasized the need to be ready for the new economy—a need to understand the forces that will likely necessitate them changing jobs, and the need to develop adaptable expertise to improve peoples' lives.

The lack of corporate-sponsored career development is a substantial threat to traditionally trained middle managers who now may neither understand nor be ready for the new employee value propositions in place today. Their jobs are less secure than at anytime in their careers, and their mind-sets and skill sets are about to atrophy. Furthermore, the racial and gender diversification of middle management is most significantly threatened by this new insecurity in spite of the reduction of traditional barriers posed by race and gender.

In the final analysis, companies are more comfortable today with promises about good pay, interesting work, and being on a team. The old days of a lifetime of employment, access to benefits, and a pension have disappeared. No doubt there are thousands of out-of-work people looking for new jobs from which they will not be fired. Unfortunately, they are looking for the kind of expansionist economy and coincidence of interests with corporate America that existed for only a brief time after the war. That was a time when there were plenty of good jobs—a time during which a well-written résumé and a few networking connections were sufficient. Today, job opportunities are flung far and wide and it is considerably more important for people to connect with the connectors, learn how to market themselves, and talk about the value they create. But even these things fall short of the more significant changes all of us will need to make.

Is it ethical to accept an offer of employment of a less than perfect job and continue looking for a better fit? In today's environment, continuing a search for better opportunities is more of a requirement rather than a question. As appropriate, companies continue to adjust their costs of labor in order to remain competitive. Failure to do so jeopardizes earnings and the long-term health of the enterprise.

Controlling costs is rational economic behavior, as is managing individual career opportunities. For individuals this means they should treat their employment opportunities rationally against the backdrop of their personal brand in the marketplace. Companies are often careful not to act callously toward workers for fear of doing damage to their employment brand. Likewise, individuals who develop reputations for being unreliable complicate their chances for reemployment. Accepting or not accepting new opportunities that come along is more a question of brand management than of ethics, and the ability to recognize the difference is an essential first step in the mind-shift process. The question of one's loyalty to a company is more reasonably viewed as a calculated economic exchange.

There are some for whom the search for employment is so urgent that now is not the time to be concerned with a shift in mind-set. One may be particularly exposed to the economic ruin that can come with catastrophic illness without having adequate health care insurance, or someone may have financial obligations requiring immediate attention. These are circumstances in which finding a job is more immediate. Readers facing these issues would find it helpful to return to the first few chapters in Part II as well as the Resources guide, and take the first reasonable job available. But do continue looking for a better fit.

The most significant adjustment individuals can make is to gain control of their job transitions, career searches, and lives. In this respect knowledge is power, but it is an engine without fuel. That is, knowledge is not enough. It must be put to use. Recall the experiences of Mary Parsons, the outplacement counselor whose twenty-four-month company orientation was interrupted. She was in the midst of living through a rather abrupt change in an employment value proposition. Her first instinct was to blame herself and ask what she could have done better to be among the few in her class to be retained. Consider Roy. His view of the world (as well as my own) led him to a dysfunctional "good-guy/bad-guy" interpretation of events.

By understanding the new context in which we live and that good jobs are available only as long as they make economic sense for companies to offer them, we are in a better position to understand and thereby take control. The most immediate use we can make of this knowledge is to understand and adjust to the reality that our jobs are for shorter durations than before. That is, be prepared for an interruption in one's monthly income stream. The notion may be simple enough, but Americans are notoriously unprepared. Practically any unanticipated uptick in expenses drives people to the edge of bankruptcy or payment delinquency. For example, in the summer of 2005 when gasoline prices spiked upward from the hurricane shortages created by Katrina, many Americans were pushed right to the economic edge. Gasoline credit card purchases at the pump rose to 70 percent of all such purchases, up from 54 percent the previous year. Delinquent credit card payments immediately spiked to a record 4.81 percent of all payments in the quarter.

In 2005 a television commercial featured a man presumptively living the good life. He is seen in front of his house, driving his expensive car and playing golf at his country club, and asks: "How can I afford all of this? I am in debt up to my eyeballs. I can barely meet the interest payments." The truly remarkable aspect of the ad was its proposed solution—borrow more money. Debt being taken on by Americans is skyrocketing both because of credit card usage and home equity lines of credit. Americans tend to confuse what someone is willing to lend them with what they can realistically afford.

They have learned to structure their lives around monthly cash flows. When an income stream is interrupted, the difference between what we can afford and what a financial institution is willing to lend us becomes clear. Not all debts are bad, and some debts are better than others. Borrowing money to purchase depreciating assets (automobiles) is almost as bad as borrowing to purchase nonassets (vacations). There is no expectation that anything said here will deter people from borrowing. But as long as people spend as much or more money than they make without significant savings, they invite economic disaster when the companies for whom they work restructure, get acquired, or otherwise rationalize their costs of labor.

The mind-set shift is one that discourages personal consumption in favor of capital preservation. Already existing public policy allows people to save pretax dollars through a variety of mechanisms including 401Ks, individual retirement accounts (IRAs), and 403Bs for not-for-profit institutions. These mechanisms, in conjunction with Social Security, have the potential to eliminate any of our concerns about reasonable levels of retirement income. If this sounds a little like pie-in-the-sky thinking, it is only because we have allowed ourselves to be conditioned by a society predicated on individual maximum consumption.

The suggestion here is that there are alternative ways to consume that rest on more realistic views of what one can truly afford given the likelihood that our income streams will be interrupted at least a couple of times during our working lives. It is not unrealistic to think that people should prepare themselves for this eventuality. For those believing otherwise, job interruptions are likely to be met with scurrying about looking for the good jobs of the past. While the odds are increasingly against finding them, this does not mean one has to accept the insecurity that comes with it.

Can any of us do anything about relying on an employer-based system for distributing health care coverage? Short of working to change public policy and/or being able to afford private insurance, the answer remains no. Except, know enough to understand what companies are saying about health care coverage. That requires understanding the American system for what it is and how it operates. It is a system that aggressively distributes coverage to relatively healthy populations of people and avoids those who need coverage the most. In order to control cost, some companies will focus on health maintenance. Others will shift cost to employees and customers. Still others will move production to locations where the cost of health care coverage is less of a problem.

The endgame is the same; cost control, and no one company is in a position to bear the cost of coverage simply because it is the right thing to do. In a flat world, companies with inefficient cost structures are at a disadvantage.

In the main, the American system of coverage is a private sector solution whose primary concerns are with profit maximization and not public health. When the two conflict, profits win most of the time. Individuals are left with two primary means of navigating the global economy: continuous upgrading of their skills to create value, and being aggressive about promoting their personal brands in the marketplace. They do this to make sure they are seen as creating value.

The concept of individual value creation may feel foreign to some because people are not used to thinking about the value they create on their jobs. It is a useful and powerful tool. Think back for a moment at the receptionist in Oakbrook and the engineering students at Northwestern. Miesha does not just do her job. She has learned how to create value. The message she conveys to a prospective employer is that from the position of the front desk, she can make a difference. In this sense she is more than a receptionist. She is the director of first impressions and someone the business relies on to manage its brand with prospective clients. In truth, the skill set through which she makes a difference is applicable across a number of positions for which she might be a candidate.

The engineering students are a slightly more complicated case. They are being told that success comes with using adaptable expertise to improve the lives of people. They must continue to improve their communications skills and ability to apply their engineering expertise across multiple domains. It is easy to see which kinds of engineers organizations are likely to want as employees.

This is where issues of race and gender are likely to recede in importance. The case of the black athlete is used to amplify the point. Once American sports were racially integrated, the unwillingness of some colleges and universities to welcome black athletes onto their campuses became a costly prejudice difficult to afford. Later, black athletes routinely were recruited to colleges and universities where they had previously been unwelcome. As athletic departmental budgets mushroomed into multimillion-dollar enterprises, the ability to recruit prize athletes had a direct economic impact on a university. The translation is this: Any time a company or institution systematically excludes people who can create value and make a difference, they have an expensive prejudice few can afford. Some of the value created comes because customers demand diversity. Other value is created because individuals bring unique skills to the workplace that are in demand and relatively scarce. Regardless, smart companies survive because they figure out how to identify, recruit, and retain talent. Smart people survive because they learn to create the value others need.

When Dan Bowman decided to accept a job offer with another company rather than open his own business, he did so because he wanted to learn everything there was to learn about running the business. He went to work fully understanding the employment proposition on the table. Paige Stewart did likewise. In that respect, they both made outstanding employees. When Dan found out that his company had been sold, he endorsed it as an opportunity rather than as a disappointment. Others, who might have been looking for something different in an employer, were undoubtedly unhappy. But Dan was ready for almost any eventuality. He knew enough to start his own business. His skills and reputation (brand) were such that others would offer him jobs as well. And it was not unreasonable to think the new company might get in line to take advantage of the value Dan is able to create. Dan had taken control in a way all of us are encouraged to do so.

Not long ago I discovered that my nephew had just about perfected the art of creating value outside the corporate structure. His job for the past ten years has been in loose partnership with others rehabbing houses and then selling them. With occasional help from his parents, he has developed an income stream that reflects the kind of job he has. That is, when he creates value, he earns money. When he doesn't, he doesn't earn money. In fact, he really does not have a job at all. There is no job description or set of parameters defining his duties. He does whatever is necessary to create value, which is directly reflected in sales. He assumes and sheds debt in a way that reflects his intermittent cash flow.

Lately, I have found myself seeking him out for his understanding of the real estate market and its risks. He recently returned from the Union of South Africa after exploring the rapidly evolving apartment and housing market there. I have no idea how successful he is or will be. But I do know he has learned to create value in an unstructured environment.

- Mary Parsons
- Michigan State University
- Dan Bowman
- Paige Stewart
- Miesha Collins
- My nephew
- The Undergraduate Engineering Department at Northwestern
- And others, I am sure.

This list is undoubtedly longer than shown here, but not nearly as long as it needs to be. It is a list of individuals and institutions I know who are uniquely positioned to survive in the new economy.

Dan Bowman and Paige Stewart have figured out how to take control of their own careers. Mary Parsons knew her skills were about to atrophy and must be updated. Miesha Collins and my nephew have learned how to create value. The Undergraduate Engineering Department at Northwestern University is teaching its students how to improve the lives of people across multiple domains. Michigan State has reached out and embraced the global economy.

For each the reality is the same: As distance dies, it opens a whole new world in which work can be done by anyone, anywhere, if they can develop the mind-set to get it done.

NOTES

CHAPTER ONE

1. Robert Reich, "Why Factory Jobs are Disappearing—All Over," Public Radio Marketplace Commentaries, broadcast November 5, 2003.

2. Thomas L. Friedman, *The World Is Flat: A Brief History of the Twenty-First Century* (New York: Farrar, Straus and Giroux, 2005), pp. 7–9.

3. Reported in numerous places including *CNN Money Report*, broadcast December 10, 2001.

4. Martha Renstrom-Plourd, "A History of the Outplacement Industry, 1960–1997" (unpublished PhD dissertation, Virginia Tech University, April 1998), pp. 28–29.

5. Department of Education data reported by Jennifer Ann Adams, "Visualizing the Changing Spatial Patterns of American Higher Education, 1940–1999" (unpublished paper presented at the annual meeting of the Association for the Study of Higher Education; Sacramento, California), November 2002.

6. Renstrom-Plourd, "History of Outplacement," pp. 28–29.

7. William Bridges, *Job Shift: How to Prosper in a Workplace without Jobs* (Cambridge, MA: Perseus Books, 1994) pp. 29–53.

8. Frances Cairncross, *The Death of Distance: How the Communications Revolution Is Changing Our Lives* (Boston: Harvard Business School Press, 1997), p. 5.

9. Barbara Ehrenreich, *Bait and Switch: The (Futile) Pursuit of the American Dream* (New York: Henry Holt, 2005), p. 218.

CHAPTER TWO

1. Jack Welch, *Straight from the Gut* (New York: Warner Books, 2001), p. 129.

2. Lou Dobbs, *Exporting America: Why Corporate Greed Is Shipping American Jobs Overseas* (New York: Warner Books, 2004).

3. *New York Times Book Review*, January 16, 2005.

CHAPTER THREE

1. Study of CEO tenure conducted by Messenger Associates, Inc., a DBM Company, February 22, 2000.

2. Eli Ginzberg and George Vojta, *Beyond Human Scale: The Large Corporation at Risk* (New York: Basic Books, 1987), p. 32.

3. Renstrom-Plourd, "History of Outplacement," p. 18.

4. See, for example, Spencer Crew, "The Great Migration of Afro-Americans, 1915–40," *Monthly Labor Review* 110 (1987).

5. Renstrom-Plourd, "History of Outplacement," p. 20.

6. Ginzberg and Vojta, *Beyond Human Scale*, p. 61.

7. Ibid., p. 80.

8. Renstrom-Plourd, "History of Outplacement," p. 37.

9. Ibid., p. 61.

10. Daniel Denzer, "The Outsourcing Bogeyman," *Foreign Affairs* (May–June 2004): p. 3.

11. John Heilmann, "The New Economy, Stupid," *Electrosphere* 203 (March 1996).

12. Cairncross, *Death of Distance*, pp. 75–98.

13. Jacob Kirkegaard, "Outsourcing and Off-Shoring: Pushing the European Model Over the Hill Rather Than Off the Cliff," working paper for the Institute for International Economics.

CHAPTER FOUR

1. Jeff Bennett and John Lippert, "Delphi Contract Offer Cuts Wages, Scraps Health Care," reported on Bloomberg.com, October 11, 2005.

2. Dobbs, *Exporting America*, pp. 7–19.

3. Bernadette Tansey, "Are Bio-Tech Jobs the Next to Go?" *San Francisco Chronicle,* April 18, 2004, p. 11.

4. Chris Isidore, "What Outsourcing?: Layoffs from Work Going Offshore Resulted in Just 2.5% of Total Layoffs in Quarter," reported on *CNN Money*, June 10, 2004.

5. Kirkegaard, "Outsourcing and Off-Shoring," pp. 14–17.

6. Mark Landler, "A German Auto Supplier Is the Un-Delphi," *New York Times*, November 24, 2005, p. C-1.

7. Reported in *Business Week*, March 21, 2005.

8. Gladwell, *Tipping Point*, pp. 133–92.

9. Ibid., pp. 164–65.

10. Ibid., p. 145.

11. Jill Quadagno, "Why the United States Has No National Health Care," *Journal of Health and Social Behavior* 45, extra issue (2004): pp. 25–44.

12. Gerald Cavanaugh, "Why America Doesn't Have Universal Health Care," *Sentient Times* (February 1999).

13. Melissa Thomasson, "Health Care Insurance in the United States," reported in *EH.Net Encyclopedia.*

14. "Blue Cross/Blue Shield of Texas: Our History," reported on BC/BS of Texas website.

15. Paul Starr, *The Social Transformation of American Medicine: The Rise of a Sovereign Profession and the Making of a Vast Industry* (New York: Basic Books), pp. 280–83.

16. Leslie Weatherly, "The Rising Cost of Healthcare," *HR* magazine (September 2004).

17. Victoria Colliver, "Middle-Class Americans Face Life without Health Insurance," *San Francisco Chronicle*, December 31, 2004.

18. McKenzie Institute Roundtable on Offshoring, featuring Ron Blackwell, Tom Friedman, Jeffrey Garten, and Dianna Farrell (moderator), 2004.

19. Ed Wolf, "The Devolution of the American Pension System: Who Gains and Who Loses," *Eastern Economic Journal* (fall 2003): p. 3.

20. Ibid., pp. 8–9.

21. Peter Capelli, "A Market-Driven Approach To Retaining Talent," *Harvard Business Review* (February 2000).

22. Friedman, *World Is Flat*, pp. 24–29.

CHAPTER FIVE

1. Reported on the website of the American College of Physicians (ACP) by their Office of Research Planning.

2. Starr, *Transformation of American Medicine*, p. 124.

3. Reported in newspapers throughout the United States and elsewhere. See, for example, "A Senate Apology for History on Lynching," *Washington Post*, June 14, 2005, p. A-12.

4. Amartya Sen, *Development as Freedom* (New York: Anchor Books, 1999), pp. 35–53.

5. *Dred Scott v. Sanford*, 19 How. 393 (1857).

6. Don Fehrenbacher, *The Dred Scott Case: Its Significance in American Law and Politics* (New York: Oxford University Press, 2001), p. 580.

7. *Dred Scott v. Sanford*.

8. *Plessy v. Ferguson*, 163 U.S. 537 (1896).

9. Ibid.

10. James Heflin's remarks came as a part of his participation in numerous filibusters on the Senate floor and came again soon after in the wake of the U.S. Senate's passage of the antilynching resolution. Cited in numerous places, including *The Christian Century*, July 26, 2005, p. 5.

11. Vernon Jordan, *Vernon Can Read!* (Cambridge, MA: Public Affairs, 2001), p. 7.

12. *Missouri ex rel. Gaines v. Canada*, 395 U.S. 337 (1938).

13. Ibid.

14. *Brown et al. v. The Board of Education of Topeka*, 347 U.S. 483 (1954).

15. Irving J. Spitzberg Jr. and Virginia Thorndike, *Creating Community on College Campuses* (Albany: State University of New York Press, 1992).

16. Ibid.

17. Ann Crittenden, *The Price of Motherhood* (New York: Henry Holt, 2002), p. 63.

18. Andrew Sum et al., "The Growing Gender Gap in College Enrollments and Degree Attainment in the United States," a report prepared for the Business Roundtable, May 2003.

19. Frances DiMaglio, "Breaking the B-School Barriers," *Business Week* (December 1, 2004).

20. Reported on CNN News, February 2003.

21. Corenne A. Marasco, "Women Under 40 Are Closing the Salary Gap," *Chemical & Engineering News* 81 (April 2003).

22. William Ferrell, *Why Men Earn More* (New York: AMACOM, 2005).

23. Crittenden, *Price of Motherhood*, pp. 24–25.

24. Ibid., p. 90.

25. Ibid., p. 108.

26. Timothy L. O'Brien, "Why Do So Few Women Reach the Top in Law Firms," *International Herald Tribune*, March 19, 2006, http://iht.com/articles/2006/03/19/business/web.0319obrien.php.

27. Elizabeth Millard, "Keeping Careers on Track—Mommy or Not," *ABA eJournal*, October 14, 2001, http://www.abanet.org/journal/ereport/oc14chicklit.html.

28. Crittenden, *Price of Motherhood*, pp. 65–66.

CHAPTER SIX

1. Gladwell, *Tipping Point.*

2. Jeffrey Fox, *Don't Send a Résumé: And Other Contrarian Rules to Help Land a Great Job* (New York: Hyperion, 2001), p. 5.

3. Cairncross, *Death of Distance*, p. 9.

4. Margaret Steen, "Older Workers Facing Tough Market," reprinted by www .TodaysSeniorNetwork.com.

CHAPTER SEVEN

1. From www.quintcareers.com.

2. Michelle Tullier, *Networking for Job Search and Career Success* (Indianapolis: JIST Publishing, 2004), p. 9.

3. Bolles, *Parachute*, p. 124.

4. Ehrenreich, *Bait and Switch*, pp. 121–47.

5. Tullier, *Networking for Job Search*, p. 9.

6. Gladwell, *Tipping Point*, p. 54.

7. John Lucht, *Rites of Passage: The Insider's Guide To Executive Job Changing* (New York: Viceroy Press, 1995).

8. Welch, *Straight from the Gut,* p. 157.

9. Jack Trout, *Differentiate or Die: Survival in Our Era of Killer Competition* (New York: John Wiley & Sons, 2000).

CHAPTER EIGHT

1. Neil D. Bernardo, "Business Failures Rise in Nearly Every Industry Sector in First Half of 1997," *Dunn and Bradstreet News,* Views and Trends.

2. Reference by www.sba.com, "Small business startups."

CHAPTER NINE

1. Interviews with Steven Carr (PhD), associate dean, Undergraduate Engineering, Northwestern University, summer 2005.

2. Ibid.

3. Interviews with Edward Colgate (PhD), director, Design Engineering, Northwestern University, fall 2005.

4. U.S. Statutes at Large 12 (1862): 503.

5. Reported in various places, including *Automotive News* (November 11, 2005).

6. See Bob Darrow, "Simon: MSU to Be a Model University, *The State News,* September 9, 2005.

7. Peter Cappelli, *The New Deal at Work* (Boston MA.: Harvard Business Press, 1999), p. 17.

8. Ibid., pp. 25–26.

9. Chad Terhune, "Wal-Mart Has Limited Plan: Fastest Growing Plan Has a Catch," *Wall Street Journal,* May 14, 2003.

10. Cappelli, *New Deal at Work*, pp. 46–48.

RESOURCES

The resources section is divided into two parts. Part I is a bibliography of books I recommend for further reading for those interested in understanding many of the issues raised mostly in the Context part of the book. They are personally recommended because of what they added to my knowledge on various subjects and not because I advocate any particular points of view they espouse. They are books that collectively provide an excellent base upon which to build your own perspective of the challenges of the new economy and associated issues.

Part II is directed primarily at those interested in "Practical Applications." It consists of readings and self-described websites by topic. They are largely resources others have directed to my attention as having been helpful to them. While I have visited every website listed here and spent time exploring their content, I am not endorsing any of them. I believe they are reputable organizations, but I am not in a position to vouch for them personally. I simply do not know each of their reputations in sufficient detail. For the websites, I have reproduced descriptive material from the organizations themselves. In the final analysis you will have to judge for yourself, but I am optimistic you will have positive experiences.

The items listed here are not intended to be exhaustive. One could easily have come up with an entirely different list. As you begin reading you will uncover additional resources. I encourage you to add them to your own personal list.

PART I: BOOKS

Beckwith, Harry. *Selling the Invisible: A Field Guide to Modern Marketing*. New York: Warner Books, 1997.

Birkeland, Peter M. *Franchising Dreams: The Lure of Entrepreneurship in America*. Chicago: University of Chicago Press, 2002.

Bolles, Richard Nelson. *What Color Is Your Parachute: A Practical Guide for Job Hunters & Career Changers*. Berkeley, CA: Ten Speed Press, 2000.

Cairncross, Frances. *The Death of Distance: How the Communications Revolution Is Changing Our Lives*. Boston: Harvard Business School Press, 1997.

Cappelli, Peter. *The New Deal at Work*. Boston: Harvard Business School Press, 1999.

Clark, Robert, and Ann McDermed. *The Choice of Pension Plans in a Changing Economy.* Washington, DC: American Enterprise Institute, 1990.

Crittenden, Ann. *The Price of Motherhood: Why the Most Important Job in the World Is Still the Least Valued.* New York: Henry Holt, 2001.

Delous, Richard S. *The Contingent Economy.* Washington, DC: National Planning Association, 1989.

Dobbs, Lou. *Exporting America: Why Corporate Greed Is Shipping American Jobs Overseas.* New York: Warner Books, 2004.

Dotlich, David, and Peter C. Cairo. *Why CEOs Fail: The 11 Behaviors That Can Derail Your Climb to the Top—And How to Manage Them.* San Francisco: John Wiley & Sons, 2003.

Downs, Alan. *Corporate Executions: The Ugly Truth about Layoffs: How Corporate Greed Is Shattering Lives, Companies, and Communities.* New York: AMACOM, 1995.

Ehrenreich, Barbara. *Bait and Switch: The (Futile) Pursuit of the American Dream.* New York: Holt and Company, 2005. See also www.barbaraehrenreich.com for opportunities to interact with other white-collar professionals.

Fox, Jeffrey. *Don't Send a Resume: And Other Contrarian Rules to Help Land a Great Job.* New York: Hyperion, 2001.

Friedman, Thomas L. *The World Is Flat: A Brief History of the Twenty-First Century.* New York: Farrar, Straus & Giroux, 2005.

Gladwell, Malcolm. *The Tipping Point: How Little Things Can Make a Big Difference.* New York: Little, Brown, 2000.

Hakim, Cliff. *We Are All Self-Employed.* San Francisco: Berrett-Koehler, 1994.

Heckscher, Charles. *White Collar Blues.* New York: Basic Books, 1995.

Jackall, Robert. *Moral Mazes: The World of Corporate Managers.* New York: Oxford University Press, 1998.

Jordan, Vernon Jr. *Vernon Can Read!: A Memoir.* New York: Public Affairs, 2001.

Lucht, John. *Rites of Passage at $100,000+.* New York: Viceroy Press, 1993.

Mackay, Harvey. *We Got Fired: And It's the Best Thing That Ever Happened to Us.* New York: Ballantine, 2004.

Murphy, Evelyn. *Getting Even: Why Women Don't Get Paid Like Men—And What to Do About It.* New York: Simon & Schuster, 2005.

Newman, Katherine S. *Falling from Grace: Downward Mobility in the Age of Affluence.* Berkeley: University of California Press, 1999.

Rifkin, Jeremy. *The End of Work: The Decline of the Global Labor Force and the Dawn of the Post-Modern Era.* New York: Putnam, 1996.

Rose, Stephen. *The Decline of Employment Stability in the 1980s.* Washington, DC: National Commission on Employment Policy, 1995.

Starr, Paul. *The Social Transformation of American Medicine: The Rise of a Sovereign Profession and the Making of a Vast Industry.* New York: Basic Books, 1982.

Trout, Jack. *Differentiate or Die: Survival in Our Era of Killer Competition.* New York: John Wiley & Sons, 2000.

Welch, Jack. *Straight from the Gut.* New York: Warner Books, 2001.

Wilson, Diane Grimard. *Back in Control: How to Stay Sane, Productive, and Inspired in Your Transition.* Boulder, CO: Sentient Publications, 2004.

PART II

According to the American Library Association there is no national directory of self-help job search groups. Such groups exist and can be resourced by calling your local public library. They are not in all public libraries, but many libraries will be able to direct you to where they exist in their respective metropolitan areas.

WOMEN'S RESOURCES

Books

Bazar, Tara, Jane Boucher, Jan Fraser, Cherie Carter-Scott, and Lisa Walker. *Ordinary Women . . . Extraordinary Success: Everything You Need to Excel, from America's Top Women Motivators*. Franklin Lakes, NJ: Career Press, 2004.

Friedman, Caitlin, and Kimberly Yorio. *The Girls' Guide to Starting Your Own Business*. New York: HarperResource, 2003.

Hadley, Joyce, and Betsy Sheldon. *The Smart Woman's Guide to Networking*. Frankin Lakes, NJ: Career Press, 1995.

Henry, Amy. Foreword by Donald Trump. *What It Takes: Speak Up, Step Up, Move Up: A Modern Woman's Guide to Success in Business*, New York: St. Martin's Press, 2004.

Johnson, Tory, Lindsey Pollak, and Robyn Freeman Spizman. *Women for Hire: The Ultimate Guide to Getting a Job*. New York: Perigee, 2002.

King, Julie Adair. *Smart Woman's Guide to Interviewing and Salary Negotiation*. Franklin Lakes, NJ: Career Press, 1995.

Websites

www.womenwork.org

"Women Work! is a membership organization dedicated to helping women from diverse backgrounds achieve economic self-sufficiency through job readiness, education, training, and employment. Women Work! provides job readiness, education, and training services through a network of more than 1,000 programs nationwide. Women Work! also takes on the toughest women's employment issues and fights for them in Congress and in state legislatures."

www.careerwomen.com

"These premier career portals are for firms of all sizes that are setting the standards for recruiting and hiring top-notch candidates in the workforce. Industry-leading technology, rich in functionality, helps employers manage the hiring life cycle easily and effectively. We are a 100 percent women-owned e-recruiting network of premier niche sites that have been helping employers find top-quality candidates to meet their growing business needs since 1996. The Career Exposure Network™ is dedicated to helping our networkwide job candidates find the best career opportunities with the best companies while helping our employers further their e-recruiting efforts, especially to our sought-after, targeted women, diversity & MBA candidates. We continually implement industry-leading technologies that will help you effectively manage the hiring process."

www.womenforhire.com

"Founded in 1999 as the first and only company devoted to a comprehensive array of recruitment services for women, Women For Hire offers signature career expos, inspiring speeches and seminars, a popular career-focused magazine, customized marketing programs, and an online job board that help leading employers connect with top-notch professional women in all fields."

www.advancingwomen.net

"WomensJobSearch.net combines the Internet's most powerful technologies into an elegant, powerful, and easy to use system. This extraordinary recruiting tool facilitates communication between hiring officials and candidates like never before. Navigation is simple and provides visitors with a wealth of valuable information, quickly and easily. A combination of simplicity and elegance makes the WomensJobSearch.net user experience unparalleled by any other job board."

www.advancingwomen.com

"Advancing Women went live on the Net in 1996 and was the first organization to fuse the power of the Net with the compelling agenda of women seeking the most effective means of advancing their career. Since 1996, Advancing Women in its various alliances has been one of the top women and diversity career sites on the Net. On January 1, 2005, Advancing Women moved on from this alliance to create its own more targeted job board, specifically to serve the needs of our own audience and employers seeking women and diversity candidates. Advancing Women also offers a special section for those women seeking executive careers in the $60K–$750K+ range."

MINORITY RESOURCES

Books

Beech, Wendy. *Black Enterprise Guide to Starting Your Own Business*. New York: John Wiley, 1999.

Bell, Edmondson, Ella L. Bell, and Stella M. Nkomo, *Our Separate Ways: Black and White Women and the Struggle for Professional Identity*. Boston: Harvard Business School Press, 2001.

Kao, Patricia, Susan Tien, and the staff of *Vault*, *Vault Guide to Conquering Corporate America: For Women and Minorities*. New York: Vault, Inc., 2003.

Stith, Anthony. *How to Build a Career in the New Economy: A Guide for Minorities and Women*. Los Angeles and Toronto: Warwick, 1999.

Websites

www.imdiversity.com

"IMDiversity.com was conceived by the *Black Collegian* magazine, which has provided African-American college students with valuable information on career and job opportunities since 1970. IMDiversity.com is dedicated to providing career and self-development information to all minorities, specifically African-Americans, Asian-Americans, Hispanic-Americans, Native Americans, and women. The goal of IMDiversity.com is to provide you with access to the largest database of equal opportunity employers committed to workplace diversity. Our mission is twofold: To help you find a job, and empower you with the tools and information you need in order to succeed at that job. To provide each group with political, economic, and spiritual information specific to their ethnic group, thus empowering them to achieve personal fulfillment. IMDiversity.com is proud to reflect the rich culture and heritage of each under-represented group in their own virtual village, which contains news and feature articles by leading writers, thinkers, academicians, politicians, and social activists."

www.corpdiversitysearch.com

"We at Corporate Diversity Search, Inc. will never underestimate the importance of your career change. We will work closely with you to ensure that your next career opportunity will challenge you, not only in your immediate new position but later on as your career progresses and you assume broader responsibilities. During the course of listening to you and asking questions, we learn what your professional and personal objectives are. It is this comprehensive approach that ultimately leads to successful job placements that position both our candidates and client companies for growth and success."

www.multiculturaladvantage.com

"Mulitculturaladvantage.com [is] an online community where minority professionals and leaders can stay informed, identify opportunities and learn firsthand what it takes to stay ahead of the pack. Included are thousands of articles, checklists, research reports, and links covering career issues, diversity, racism, ESL, immigration, education, business and other topics of interest to minorities and people working with multicultural issues. The Multicultural Advantage provides news & commentary, fresh information, viewpoints and experiences every business day from people of color working in the trenches.

The Multicultural Advantage provides timely coverage of workplace and education issues and trends relevant to minorities in fields from all backgrounds and from every level—from student to CEO. It also contains in-depth how-to articles designed to help our readers grow and succeed. The site also provides resources for companies that seek to become more effective with diversity staffing."

www.hirediversity.com

"HireDiversity.com is the nation's leading online service for diversity recruitment and career development. HireDiversity.com provides top-quality services and networking opportunities while linking underrepresented candidates with *Fortune* 1000 Corporations, government agencies, and nonprofit/educational institutions. We support the career development and success of job candidates from all levels of experience, from seasoned multicultural professionals to college graduates to interns. Many of our clients operate in a global economy or industry sector that seeks highly skilled, multicultural, and/or bilingual professionals that can best represent them in their respective target markets. HireDiversity.com offers the largest full spectrum diversity database in the industry. Services include custom memberships, résumé access, job posting, and corporate branding campaigns utilizing online & print advertising. Our customer service department is here to assist you with your hiring efforts by providing pre-screened, entry- to senior-level, diversity professionals."

www.quintcareers.com/diversity
"Quintessential Careers is the ultimate career, job, and college site, offering free expert career and job-hunting advice (through articles, tools, tips, and tutorials) as well as links to all the best job sites. Special sections for teens, college students, and all other job-seekers (by industry, geography, and job-seeker type) makes this site a comprehensive resource for all. Now with more than 2,200 pages of career and job-hunting content."

RÉSUMÉS

Books

Bennett, Scott. *The Elements of Résumé Style: Essential Rules and Eye-Opening Advice for Writing Résumés and Cover Letters that Work.* Amacom, 2005.
Betrus, Michael, and Jay A. Block. *101 Best Resumes: Endorsed by the Professional Association of Resume Writers.* New York: McGraw-Hill, 1997.
Greene, Brenda. *Get the Interview Every Time: Fortune 500 Hiring Professionals' Tips for Writing Winning Résumés and Cover Letters.* Chicago: Dearborn Trade Publishing, 2004.
Hizer, David, David V. Hizer, and Arthur Rosenberg. *The Resume Handbook: How to Write Outstanding Resumes and Cover Letters for Every Situation.* Boston: Bob Adams, 1985.
Hofferber, Karen, and Kim Issacs. *The Career Change Resume: How to Reinvent Your Resume and Land Your Dream Job.* New York: McGraw-Hill, 2003.
Jackson, Tom. *The Perfect Resume: Today's Ultimate Job Search Tool.* New York: Broadway Books, 2004.
Leifman, Howard. *Vault Guide to Resumes, Cover Letters & Interviewing: Master Three Keys to a Fruitful Job Search.* New York: Vault, 2003.

Websites

www.write-a-resume.org
"Write-A-Resume is dedicated to providing clear, useful information about resume-writing for individuals who are seeking a job or progressing toward their career goals. Our hope is to empower individuals by providing useful and informative tips for preparing a professional resume. Individuals who are seeking an improved work environment or simply advancing in their careers are encouraged to visit this site often."

www.how-to-write-a-resume.org

"The mission of How To Write A Resume.org is to assist a job-seeker with how to write a resume and cover letter, distributing a resume to hiring managers, and assistance for composing a thank you letter. How To Write A Resume.org was designed for everyone from the novice job-hunter to the HR professional. Please enjoy How To Write A Resume.org, and e-mail us by clicking on 'contact us' if you have any questions or comments on how to make a resume."

www.rockportinstitute.com/resumes

"Founded in 1981, the Rockport Institute has coached more mid-career professionals through career change than any other organization. Rockport has created many of the methods used by leading-edge career counseling professionals and has brought the art of choosing a fulfilling career into the twenty-first century.

We offer programs and services to people of all ages and situations. Clients have one thing in common: a desire to make a career choice that will be highly satisfying and lead to maximum success."

STARTING YOUR OWN BUSINESS

Books

Harper, Stephen C. Foreword by Fred DeLuca. *The McGraw-Hill Guide to Starting Your Own Business: A Step-by-Step Blueprint for the First-Time Entrepreneur*. New York: McGraw-Hill, 2003.

Keup, Erwin J. *Franchise Bible: How to Buy a Franchise or Franchise-Own Business*. Irvine, CA: Entrepreneur Press, 2004.

Leibowitz, Martin L. *Franchise Value: A Modern Approach to Security Analysis*. Hoboken, NJ: John Wiley & Sons, 2004.

Lesonsky, Rieva, and *Entrepreneur* magazine. *Start Your Own Business: The Only Start-Up Book You'll Ever Need*. Irvine, CA: Entrepreneur Press, 2001.

Norman, Jan. *What No One Ever Tells You about Starting Your Own Business: Real-Life Start-Up Advice from 101 Successful Entrepreneurs*. Chicago: Dearborn Trade Publishing, 2005.

Tomzack, Mary E. *Tips & Traps when Buying a Franchise*. Oakland: Source Book Publications, 1999.

Websites

www.smallbizbooks.com

"Providing essential business information to help plan, run, and grow your business. *Entrepreneur* magazine's SmallBizBooks.com was first launched in 1997. Since then our site has grown to include Entrepreneur Press books and software. SmallBizBooks.com is part of Entrepreneur Media. For over twenty years, Entrepreneur Media has offered a full range of products and services to entrepreneurs so that they have the relevant information they need to make informed decisions."

www.entrepreneur.com
"Whether you need help writing a business plan or marketing plan, finding a franchise or business opportunity, starting a home-based business, or building a *better* business, our extensive how-tos will lead you through the process. Free, thorough, and easy to use, these learning tools are essential to starting and growing your business."

www.alistapart.com/articles/startingabusiness (article)

FINANCING A START-UP

Books

American Bar Association, ABA, *American Bar Association Legal Guide for Small Business: Everything a Small-Business Person Must Know, from Start-up to Employment Laws to Financing and Selling a Business*. New York: Three Rivers Press, 2000.

Fisherman, Stephen. *Working for Yourself: Law and Taxes for Independent Contractors, Freelancers, and Consultants*. Berkeley, CA: Nolo, 2002.

Spinelli, Stephen, Jeffrey A. Timmons, and Andrew Zacharakis. *How to Raise Capital: Techniques and Strategies for Financing and Valuing Your Small Business*. New York: McGraw-Hill, 2005

WRITING A BUSINESS PLAN

Books

Abrams, Rhonda M., Eugene Kleiner, and contribution by Andrew Anker. *Successful Business Plans: Secrets and Strategies*. Palo Alto, CA: Running 'R' Media, 2000.

DeThomas, Art, and Lin Grensing-Pophal. *Writing a Convincing Business Plan*. Hauppauge, NY: Barron's Educational Series, 2001.

McKeever, Mike. *How to Write a Business Plan*. 7th Edition. Berkeley, CA: Nolo, 2005.

Sutton, Garrett. Foreword by Robert T. Kivosaki. *Rich Dad's Advisors: The ABCs of Writing Winning Business Plans: How to Prepare a Business Plan That Others Will Want to Read—And Invest In*. New York: Warner Business Books, 2005.

GENERAL JOB SEARCH

Books

Hemming, Allison. *Work It! How to Get Ahead, Save Your Ass, and Land a Job in Any Economy*. New York: Fireside, 2003.

Wilson, Robert F. Foreword by Hinda Miller. *Executive Job Search Handbook: All You Need to Make Your Move—From Marketing Yourself with a Master Resume to*

Networking, Targeting Companies, and Negotiating the Job Offer. Franklin Lakes, NJ: Career Press, 2003.

Websites

www.vault.com

"There's a reason why *Fortune* recently called Vault 'The best place on the Web to prepare for a job search.' Job-seekers and professionals have discovered that Vault is the Internet's ultimate destination for insider company information, advice, and career management services. Vault's unique career content and services include:

Carefully researched and continually updated 'insider' information on over 3,000 companies and 70 industries. (Called 'edgy, fun reads' by *Forbes*)."

www.careerjournal.com

"CareerJournal.com is the Internet's premier career site for executives, managers, and professionals. The site's job database offers more than 100,000 available positions, including job listings in the CareerJournal National Network, a database containing opportunities from *local and national newspaper, magazine, and TV station websites* across the United States. CareerJournal's resume database offers the most confidential access on the Web and provides candidates with flexibility and security in posting their credentials online. And CareerJournal's unlimited JobSeek Agents will alert candidates whenever a job is added that matches their criteria."

AFTER COLLEGE

Books

Adams, Bob, and Laura Morin. *The Complete Resume & Job Search Book for College Students.* Holbrook, MA: Adams Media, 1999.
Asher, Donald. *How to Get Any Job with Any Major: Career Launch and Re-Launch for Everyone Under 30 (or How to Avoid Living in Your Parents' Basement).* Berkeley: Ten Speed Press, 2004.
Krueger, Brian D. *College Grad Job Hunter: Insider Techniques and Tactics for Finding a Top-Paying Entry Level Job.* Holbrook, MA: Adams Media, 1998.

Websites

www.aftercollege.com

"AfterCollege is the largest career network specializing in recruitment at the college level. AfterCollege maintains an exclusive network of over 1,200 partnering academic departments and student groups as well as a proprietary database of over 15,000 faculty and student group contacts at the nation's top universities. Through its network, AfterCollege delivers targeted employer content to a diverse audience of students. These students range from undergraduates to PhDs, 95% of whom have bachelor's degrees or higher and 84% having GPAs of 3.0 or above."

www.collegegrad.com

"At CollegeGrad.com, we are the best at what we do. However, we are NOT trying to be everything to everyone. We provide one service and one service only:

We have been consistently profitable every year since our founding.

We are 100% internally funded by our operations, with no external debt or equity funding."

NETWORKING (CONNECTING)

Books

Darling, Diane. *The Networking Survival Guide: Get the Success You Want by Tapping into the People You Know*. New York: McGraw-Hill, 2003.

Flippen, Edward J. *Practical Networking: How to Give and Get Help with Jobs*. Authorhouse, 2001.

MacKay, Harvey. *Dig Your Well Before You're Thirsty: The Only Networking Book You'll Ever Need*. New York: Currency/Doubleday, 1997.

Tullier, Michelle L. *Networking for Job Search and Career Success*. Indianapolis: JIST Works, 2004.

NEGOTIATING

Books

Miller, Lee M. *Get More Money on Your Next Job: 25 Proven Strategies for Getting More Money, Better Benefits, and Greater Job Security*. New York: McGraw-Hill, 1998.

Northcraft, Gregory B., and Robin L. Pinkley. *Get Paid What You're Worth: The Expert Negotiator's Guide To Salary and Compensation*. New York: St. Martin's Press, 2000.

Simon, Charnan, and Mary B. Simon. *Negotiate Your Job Offer: A Step-by-Step Guide To a Win-Win Situation*. New York: Wiley, 1998.

Wendleton, Kate. *Interviewing and Salary Negotiation: For Job Hunters, Career Changers, Consultants, and Freelancers* (The Five O'Clock Club Series). Franklin Lakes, NJ: Career Press, 1999.

INTERVIEWING

Books

Fry, Ron. *101 Great Answers To the Toughest Interview Questions*. Hawthorne, NJ: Career Press, 1994.

Gottesman, Deb, and Buzz Mauro. *The Interview Rehearsal Book: Seven Steps to Job-Winning Interviews Using Acting Skills You Never Knew You Had*. New York: Berkeley Books, 1999.

Hough, Lee, Neil M. Yeager, and Neil Yeager. *Power Interviews: Job-Winning Tactics from Fortune 500 Recruiters*. New York: John, Wiley, 1998.

Veruki, Peter, and Peter Venki. *The 250 Job Interview Questions You'll Most Likely Be Asked...And the Answers That Will Get You Hired*. New York: John Wiley, 1998.

INDEX

About the Author

R. WILLIAM (BILL) HOLLAND is the principal owner of R. William Holland Consulting, LLC, a human resources consulting firm specializing in executive coaching, career management and executive team alignment. An award-winning educator, scholar, and business executive, he has served on the faculties of the University of California and Michigan State University and in executive positions for Accenture (Andersen Consulting), PepsiCo, Charles Schwab, the University of Pennsylvania, and Right Management Consulting. He has served on the boards of directors for several organizations, including the Pennsylvania Partnership for Children, The Greater Philadelphia Area YMCA, and the Chicagoland Chamber of Commerce. He is currently a founding board member of United Professionals, a not-for-profit advocacy group for under-employed and unemployed white-collar workers, and also serves as a member of the BeamPines executive coaching advisory board.